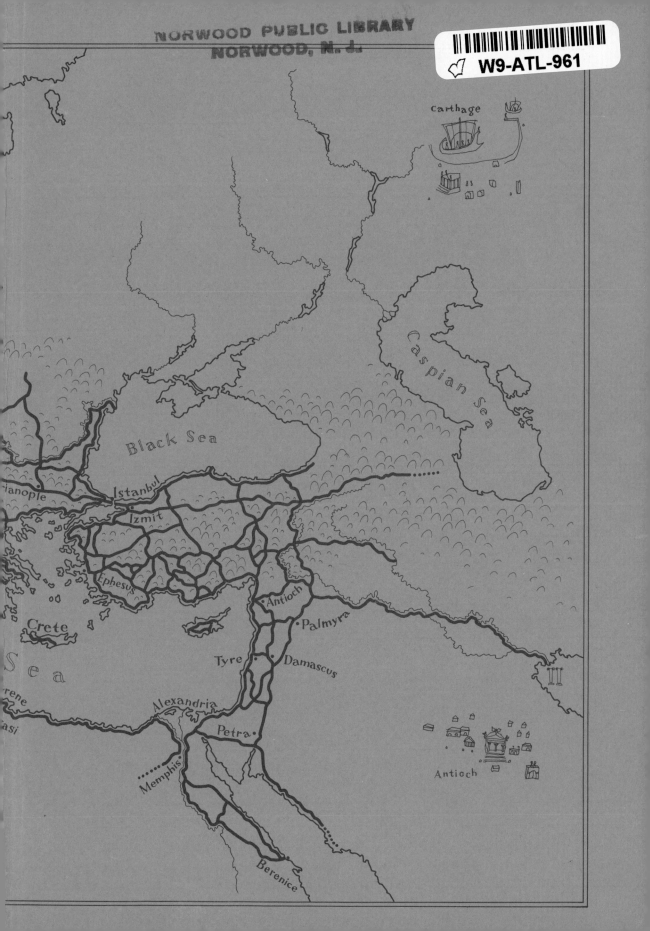

Carthage

Black Sea

Caspian Sea

Crete

Sea

rianople

Istanbul

Izmit

Ephesus

Antioch

Palmyra

Tyre

Damascus

Alexandria

Petra

Memphis

Antioch

Berenice

rene

asi

ROMAN ROADS

ROMAN ROADS

VICTOR W. VON HAGEN

PHOTOGRAPHS BY ADOLFO TOMEUCCI
ROMAN ROAD EXPEDITION

MAPS AND DRAWINGS BY DINO RIGOLO

THE WORLD PUBLISHING COMPANY
CLEVELAND AND NEW YORK

Published by The World Publishing Company
2231 West 110th Street, Cleveland 2, Ohio
Published simultaneously in Canada by
Nelson, Foster & Scott Ltd.
Library of Congress catalog card number: 65-22154
Third Impression
Copyright © 1966 by Victor W. von Hagen
Designed by Jack Jaget

For all the children of the
American Cooperative School
in Tunis, North Africa, in
whose classroom part of this
book was written

V.W.v.H.

Begun April 1964 in Tunis.
Finished 1965 in Rome.

Contents

ROMAN ROADS

I

The Via Praenestina, which went from Rome to Palestrina (Praeneste), Italy

Appius the Blind

The story of the Roman roads begins, strangely enough, with a river. It begins at the point where the Tiber River was shallow enough at times to ford. The place where traffic crossed it became a focal point. When the water was too deep, the river was crossed by boat, then in time by a bridge. From that single bridge a people marched to empire. In three hundred years the Romans conquered all Italy, and the entire known world. And what lands they conquered they covered with roads—53,000 miles of roads—one of the finest monuments man has ever left of himself.

But the early Romans had no dream of empire. The daily problem of living was quite enough. The daily struggle to grow and harvest wheat to make bread and porridge, and to find salt to season and preserve their food took up most of Roman time.

The Romans were like most tribes living in Italy. They were only one of the many that dotted the land, speaking different languages and worshiping different gods. However,

15

Ruins of Capua, terminus of the road built by Appius Claudius in 312 B.C.

to it roads. The Greeks traveled over tracks, hoping that the shuffle of men's feet and the chopping of horses' hoofs might make a road. The Persians had roads, but the Romans then did not know anything of them. India, too, had roads; Alexander the Great had found them there ". . . thronging with the king's business . . ."

But in Rome the only gravel road was the Via Salaria, or salt road, which went to the mountains. For two hundred years, even though Rome was close to the sea, the sea as a source of salt was closed to them. The Samnites had denied them the right to take salt from the sea.

So in 312 B.C., in the four hundred forty-first year after the founding of Rome, Appius appealed to the Senate: the time had come to build a road worthy of the people of Rome. Their legions had defeated the Samnites and taken their capital, Capua, 132 miles to the south. Appius urged the Senate to build Rome's first formal road from Rome to Capua. It was agreed. Few, very few, said no to Appius, for he was stubborn and self-willed.

"That year of 312 B.C. was marked," someone later remembered, "by the famous censorship of Appius Claudius . . . his memory is cherished by posterity because he built a road . . ."

In that year, Roman engineers, using soldiers as laborers, laid down the first miles of the new road over what had been a dirt road to Alba Longa, south of Rome. The Romans expected that it would carry much traffic, including oxcarts weighing as much as twelve hundred pounds, so Appius insisted that the engineers must prepare a foundation for the road. This had never been done before. The road was to be fifteen feet wide. Earth had to be dug out to a depth of three feet, then the excavation had to be filled with loose stone. On top of this were to be laid large, well-fitting, many-sided stones. These were to be fitted together without cement and

The Via Appia near the walls of Rome

so closely laid that a knife could not be inserted between them.

Though the road from Rome to Capua was to be only 132 miles long, it was the beginning of the Roman road system. Over a period of five hundred years, the Romans were to build thousands of miles of all-weather roads that one day would stretch from the Atlantic Ocean across Europe to the Black Sea, and later on as far off as the Euphrates River.

The first road was called the Via Appia, after Appius. After that time most Roman roads were named after the men who proposed, built, or financed them, or after the city or place to which the road led. The Via Appia was named after Appius Claudius Caecus, the Via Flaminia after the censor Flaminius, and the Via Salaria was named after the salt licks northeast of Rome. Via Praenestina ran to ancient Praeneste, an Etruscanized city, and the Via Ostiensis was the road that ran from Rome to its main port, Ostia, at the mouth of the Tiber.

Appius had insisted that the first road be solidly built. Rome's rivals on Italian soil, the Etruscans, had roads. But the paving they used had not been strong enough.

The Roman builders used material close at hand—the hard, basaltic lava that had once poured out of the volcanoes, hardened into a gray-black basalt stone, and that lay in huge quarries. Most of the volcanoes had been inactive since 1000 B.C., but during a period of activity they had poured out rivers of molten, liquid stone. This was to become the famous Roman silex-lava stone.

The silex was quarried, loaded on heavy solid-wheeled

The Via Praenestina, still used by local farmers, parallels a modern road

Detail of the Via Praenestina. The volcanic stones were diamond-shaped on their reverse sides and were fitted into a gravel fill to prevent them from rocking.

oxcarts, and brought to the road, where hundreds of workers were employed to cut it, shape it, and wedge it into place. And so well was it done that when a Greek, in A.D. 535, walked over the Via Appia, eight hundred years after it had been laid down, though it had been neglected, he was astonished by it: ". . . Appius had the stones planed and polished and cut them so as to form eight angles. He joined them together without cement and so closely that they do not seem to be jointed, but to form one whole; and notwithstanding the long time elapsed (847 years) and the fact of their daily being traveled over by so many vehicles and cattle, the compactness of the stones has not been lessened."

By the time the Via Appia was being laid out, the Romans had practical engineers. They were called *architecti*. In very early Rome everyone had been his own architect and his own pathmaker. Now solid and noble buildings began to appear in Rome. A forum where people could make requests for justice, markets, and temples, all stone-built, rose from the planning of an *architectus*.

Surveyors worked under the engineers. They used an instrument called a *groma*, which was a pair of boards fastened together to make a right-angled cross. Plumb lines hung down from it, and by looking through the crosspieces the surveyor could mark down a straight line.

The Via Appia went as straight as the land would permit. And as fast as the road was laid down Appius ordered the people to plant trees close to it, so as to shade those who traveled on it.

The first miles of road over the rolling lands did not cause the engineers much trouble. It was when the land began to descend toward the lowlands of Campania that their prob-

Detail of the Via Appia

A model of the groma *used by the Roman soldier-surveyor in the Museo della Civiltà Romana in Rome. The model is based on a drawing found at Pompeii.*

lems began. From the vine-covered hills above one can gaze upon the sea and upon sprawling Lake Pontia lying in the flat, warm lands of Campania.

This was the land the Romans had long sought. Once they had captured it, the open fields became pastures for their cattle and for the hogs that gave them the "plain Roman roast pork." But the trouble here was the Pontia and the vast swamps about it, called the Pontine Marshes. The Romans were used to living on the wind-swept hills of Rome. Here in the marshes the air was "damp and gross" and brought on malaria.

The Pontine Marshes began beyond a place called the Three Taverns, on the Via Appia. Here began the overflow from Lake Pontia. When the water poured down from the hills beyond and above, it flooded the countryside. The

engineers decided to build a causeway across the marshes.
The road had to be raised six feet above the flatlands so
that it would not be flooded and so that it would act as a
dike to the lake. First they drove in thick wooden piles, then
the spaces between these were filled with loose rock, and
this was tamped down with gravel. On that solid base they
set the pavement of polygonal rocks, the famous green-black
volcanic stones.

When the water became too deep, the Appian Way could
not continue. It stopped at Forum Appii. Here travelers
had either to take a small boat, usually at night, and be
pulled down the channel by mules, who walked on a narrow bank for a distance of twenty miles, or if not were ". . .
forced to make a large compass about it, so as to bring them
to Terracina."

Horace, the famous Roman poet, making his way down
the Via Appia in the year 38 B.C., stopped at Forum Appii.
He remembered the "forum jammed with boatmen and
sharp-fingered innkeepers." He decided on the boat trip.
"Now," he wrote as he lay down on the barge, "night was
preparing to spread her darkness on earth, to station stars
in the heavens." But in the morning he found that the boatmen had gone to sleep and they were at the same spot as
the night before.

Many Roman consuls and later the emperors tried to
drain the marshes. Julius Caesar brought a plan before the
Senate, but he was murdered before the project could be
started. It was not until Trajan became emperor in A.D. 98
that any serious work on draining was begun. His work
there, said an ancient writer, may be compared to Hercules'
labor in cutting off the heads of the Hydra. For until Trajan's
engineers worked to dam it, the marshes were only a series
of channels. The largest was navigable. It ran from Forum

Appii down to Terracina (Tarracina), ". . . so we may say it was a miraculous w ˉk in filling up that troublesome marsh like another Hercules; forcing up the road by great and spacious banks to bear the burden of the immense stones and weight of the Appian Way."

The Via Appia came to the sea at Terracina. There, where the mountains met the sea, was the city. From Terracina the Via Appia climbed up, zigzagging back and forth until it reached level ground, then it went around the side of the mountain. The place on top was called Anxur. Horace said that he and his party ". . . took the rest of the day to arrive at the village of Anxur, where it was loftily poised on its limestone cliffs."

In Trajan's time, when the road was rebuilt, engineers cut away the side of the mountain close to the sea so that the road could pass at sea level. And in their pride they measured off every twenty feet and marked the cut wall in Roman numerals.

Further, in the Via Appia's southward direction, the Romans again had to worry about water—the inland lake of Fondi. The Romans did not have the techniques to build a road over the deep, marshy ground between lake and sea, so from the sea they turned the road inland toward the town of Fondi (Fundi). They kept the road close to the hills. Then, after making a detour about the lake, the Via Appia came back to the sea again at the next town, Formia (Formiae), a lovely place, where the great Roman orator Cicero built his villa.

Close to the sea the road came to a temporary halt at the Liri River. There was no way to go around it. It had to be bridged. Roman soldiers were trained to swim, and they had to know how to cross rivers loaded down with their fighting gear. So under the directions of their engineers they entered the water, searching for a solid rock base onto which the first stone piles could be constructed. They designed the bridge with four arches, and built it of flat-backed brick. Only metal could have withstood the fury of the river for long, and many times during the following hundreds of years the bridge had to be rebuilt. The bridge was fully rebuilt for the last time by the order of the Emperor Domitian, who ruled from A.D. 81 to 96.

The Romans built the city of Minturno (Minturnae) close to the bridge. It was a miniature of Rome. The city had wide paved streets and a large amphitheater that still survives. Water was brought to Minturno from the hills by means of an aqueduct, parts of which also still stand. The water was carried to the houses and to the public fountains by lead pipes.

Once the river had been crossed, the Via Appia went down the coast. The sea was so near that the roar of its crashing on the shore could be heard by the travelers on the road. At a distance marked later by a Roman milestone that read CXVIII, or 118 Roman miles from the Forum in Rome, the road came to Sinuessa, in an area famous for its wine and hot sulphur baths. Here, as the terminus of the road was to be Capua, it turned sharply to the east, keeping to the high ground on the northern side of the Volturno River. Only when the road came to the outskirts of the ancient city of Capua was it necessary to cross the rapidly flowing Volturno. A bridge was constructed with three massive arches and covered with a stone called travertine. Then the road was laid upon it and went on to Capua.

Capua was an ancient Etruscan city with large buildings, most of which are in ruins. In the year 300 B.C., Capua was the terminus of the Via Appia; later the road was extended south to Benevento. Capua was very important to the Romans. Many dirt tracks that one day would be paved roads entered

Detail of the ruins of the amphitheater at Capua

the city, which was important for its markets and for its manufacture of copper objects.

By the time the road had reached Capua, Appius, its creator, was completely blind. He never lived to see his road completed to Capua, but he lived to feel it. It is said that he walked the road barefoot, so that he could feel the joints of the stones and know if they were correctly placed.

Appius's family built a large tomb for him beside the road that was named after him. That set the fashion. After that, many famous people built their tombs beside the Via Appia. Some of the tombs, as large as public buildings, held the remains of a whole family.

Most tombs were covered with marble and bore effigies of the dead. Funerals were held at night. Men came bearing torches and lighted up the road. Having built an immense wood fire, they cremated the body. It was burned as an offering to the gods, and they believed that at the same time the soul rose to the stars. Then the ashes were placed in the tomb. Then as now, going along the Via Appia one can read the inscriptions on the tombs.

On one tomb is written: ". . . *Hic Soror et Frater* . . . A weeping father mourns the untimely death of a son and a daughter. He had hoped to precede them to this tomb, according to nature's laws. Now it has been his sad fate to light their own funeral pyre. He pleads with the gods to grant that he may soon be reunited with them."

It was the custom for people to walk along the Appian Way, so later sidewalks were added. In the narrowed light of a Roman evening, people could read the inscriptions on the resting places of the great. Tombs continued southward on the Via Appia for as far as 120 miles.

It took more than 500 years to complete the Via Appia to its planned end at the port of Brundisium, modern Brindisi,

A Roman tombstone found on the Via Appia where it enters Capua

at the end of the "boot" of Italy. By that time, most of Italy had been crisscrossed with fine all-weather roads. The Punic Wars, which extended over 118 years, took most of Rome's resources, and delayed the completion of the Via Appia down to Brindisi. It was not until A.D. 114 that Trajan began the second part of the Via Appia, which carried the road two hundred miles farther on to Brindisi.

The second section began in the town of Benevento, or, as it was called then, Beneventum, the largest city south of Capua. It stands high on the hills and was known for its good air, hence its name.

"Trajan built," wrote a historian, "and extended the same Appian Way, a great road beginning at Benevento and running to Brindisi for two hundred Roman miles. This information appears on an inscribed stone and expresses handsomely how 'The Emperor Caesar . . . Trajan . . . in the year VI of his reign began the road from Beneventum to Brundisium.' "

And, to mark it, a very handsome triumphal arch was put up in Benevento, dedicated to the Emperor Trajan. It still stands today and leads to an ancient Roman bridge.

Trajan wanted to preserve the name of Via Appia even though it was he who built the last part of the road. At first, the milestones that were placed along the road read *Appia-Traiana*, then, as the road moved along southward, it became the "Way of Trajan."

In Brindisi, at the end of the 366 miles of road, Trajan placed two large columns facing the harbor and the sea. One of these proud monuments, which marked the end of the Via Appia, the queen of ancient roads, still stands.

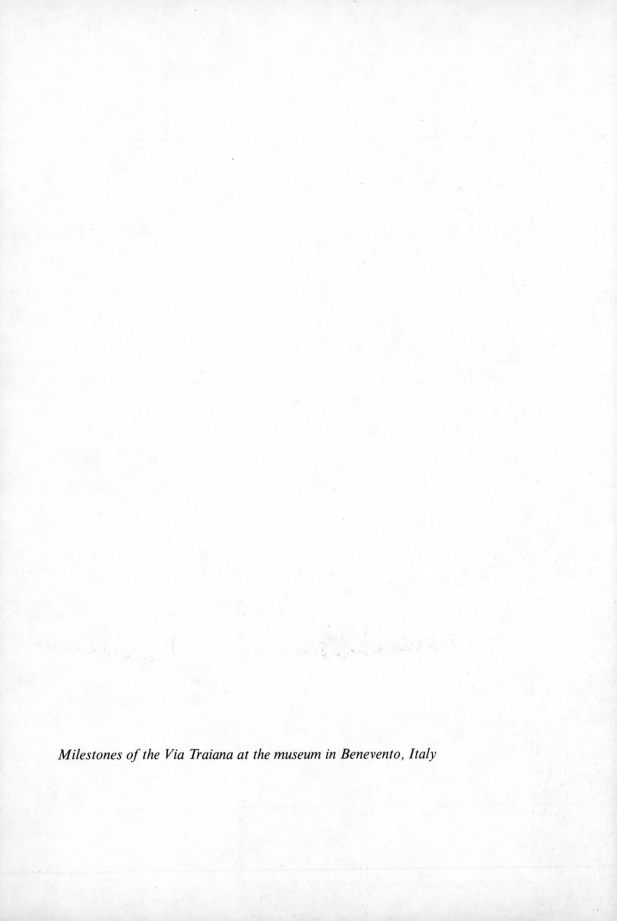

Milestones of the Via Traiana at the museum in Benevento, Italy

The Latium-Campania
Is Open

The Romans called it "the fields."

These were flatlands, crossed by numerous rivers; rich, fertile land. The Latium-Campania lay at the base of the mountains, and spread from Ostia, at the mouth of the Tiber, to Naples. In these lands the Romans settled the landless as well as old soldiers with honorable discharges from the army. The Via Appia opened the area to travel.

Soon villages were connected by country roads to the stone-paved Via Appia. They were earth roads. If there was much rain, the peasants surfaced the earth road with gravel. It became, in their words, a *via vicina*, a local road.

Along these small feeder roads houses sprang up. The Roman peasant house was usually built by a man and his neighbors. It began as a simple building, large as a barn, with rooms at either end, and the center was used to shelter the livestock. The walls were made of fieldstone, plastered

33

and whitened. The roofs were made of large red tiles. Such tiles still exist, many of them stamped with the names of those who made them.

As time went by, if the farmer-soldier did well in his farming, he turned his simple house into a villa. Then he formed his house around a courtyard. The principal rooms were in the central part, made up of sleeping quarters and a bath. In the kitchen cooking was usually done over a charcoal fire, and there were pantries and storerooms. In the veranda was the *cisterna*, an underground well that collected the water running off the clean roofs. This was the water supply for each house, so the family need not go to the public well each day to draw water.

Model of a typical Roman house in Campania, from the Museo della Civiltà Romana. The large jars held oil or wine.

Campania was ideal for wheat. Wheat was the staple of the Romans and their main worry was to get enough of it, so there was always a lively market for it. In addition to wheat, most farmers planted a vineyard. Many planted olive trees and set wheat among the growing trees. Some raised vegetables: cabbages, onions, lettuce, garlic, turnips, parsnips.

Romans bedded early. Lamps were poor things that burned olive oil and were not as good as candles. The Roman farmer rose at sunrise and had a light meal of porridge made from boiled wheat to which honey was added. Although they knew of sugar cane, it came from afar and no one but the rich could afford it. Even then sugar cane was used only for medicine.

When the farmer-soldier went off to the weekly market at the Forum Appii, he traveled over gravel roads, ten feet wide, until he reached the Via Appia. It was alive with people and movement. The Forum Appii was both a market and a place for official business. Trade brought farmers into it from widely scattered villages. Many brought their wheat in sacks to be ground into flour, for unless he had a large family and were rich enough to have slaves, a farmer did not mill his own wheat. A miller had a rotary grist mill made of rough volcanic stone and shaped like an hourglass. A farmer brought his wheat to a central locality such as the Forum Appii, where there were several mills. The quern, or mill, was turned by means of a long lever inserted into the large grinding stone and pushed either by manpower or mules. Wheat was poured into the top, and it sifted down until it filtered into the mill, where it was crushed into flour by the closely fitting millstones. The flour poured out from the lower conical stone. Many of these rotary mills still exist.

The surplus wheat not needed for a family was used for trade. Businessmen journeyed down to the Forum Appii—

it was only two days' journey from Rome—to buy wheat. Cereals were Rome's first necessity, and for a while Campania could supply Rome, but as the city grew, so grew its appetite. In time ten million bushels of wheat would be imported yearly from Africa, and five million additional bushels from Egypt.

Wheat was distributed free to the people by the Roman rulers. The man in charge of traffic on the Via Appia, which carried a huge swarm of creaking carts, was kept busy. No wagon was allowed to carry more than twelve hundred pounds, and each driver had to carry a certificate to that effect.

The weekly market in Campania on the new Via Appia was important for more than trade. Here the *aediles*, those who had charge of the public markets, brought news of the outside world to those who lived on isolated farms. The Romans had no newspapers as we know them, but after 59 B.C. they did have an official *acta diurna*, daily acts of social and political importance. All these, handwritten by scribes, reached Campania and were read to the farmers who came to trade and to hear the latest news.

With the cereals, fruits, wine, olives, and all else produced on their farms, the farmers could trade for that which they did not produce. First, salt; of all tastes, salt was vital. Grain eaters, such as the Romans were, had to have it. Soldiers who were now farmers could remember when they were given an allowance in salt; they called it the "white salary."

Salt was now taken from the sea near the port of Ostia, where the Romans were building a huge harbor to hold the trade ships coming from all over the world. A dirt road passed along the shore of the Campagna under the pine trees that grew close to the sea. Later the Emperor Severus built a fine wide road, laid with stone, connecting Terracina with

A Roman lighthouse and ships are pictured in mosaics from the offices of the merchants in Ostia, the port of the city of Rome.

Ostia. It ran along the shore for one hundred eighteen miles and connected the Via Appia with the port.

As roads developed, so did the towns in Campania. All this grew out of the fact of the Via Appia. The Romans kept adding roads that connected to it. One was called the Via Campana. It began in the town of Capua, to which Appius the Blind had first directed the Via Appia. It was a branch road. It traveled fifty miles, beautifully paved — it still exists — and went down to the port of Naples (Neapolis).

Naples had once been a Greek trading center and had a natural harbor, the best on the coast. It had one disadvantage, the dangerous and active volcano, Vesuvius. By day, a thin cloud of smoke rose out of it; at night the burning lava could be seen, as red as a steel furnace. The Roman engineers enlarged two natural harbors north of Naples. Here ships came

Road ruts in the streets of Pompeii, buried in the eruption of Vesuvius in A.D. *79, have helped archaeologists to determine the width of the wheels used in Roman transport.*

to pick up the products of Campania and in turn brought the people luxuries from other lands. There was so much traffic of wagons and chariots, and of people being carried or walking, that Augustus, when emperor, ordered his architect, named Cocceius, to eliminate the bottleneck. This he did by boring two tunnels: one at Cumae, a very sacred spot for both Greeks and Romans, and one between Pozzuoli (Puteoli) and Naples. Driven through rock, the tunnels were ten feet wide and nine feet high. They are still standing as the architects made them and are still in use.

Then finally, Campania, those wide and fertile fields stretched along between the Tyrrhenian Sea and the mountains, was given another road. In A.D. 81 the Emperor Domitian came to rule. He had been a famous soldier. He knew the value of good roads and well-made bridges and stops along the way where people could rest, eat, and slake their thirst against the summer's heat.

He had his engineers plan a new road to link with the Via Appia where it left the coast at Sinuessa and turned inland toward Capua. He had them build the road southward from Sinuessa to Naples along the coast. It was a hundred miles in length and was called the Via Domitiana after the emperor who built it. Parts of the road can still be seen today.

The building of this road that opened lower Campania was so well known that it was celebrated in a poem; the poet Statius must have seen them at work, for he writes:

> First comes the task of preparing the ditches,
> Marking the borders,
>   and, as deep as needed,
> Cutting into the earth.
> Then, second, with other stuff,

The Via Domitiana at Cumae near Naples. The old Roman stones have been surfaced with tar but appear distinctly when the road is wet.

    making a base for the crown of the highway
So that the soil does not sink
    on weakly made foundations
That give the flagstones a false base.
Thirdly, they secure it with cobblestones,
Closely packed.
Now see how many hands are working together.
Some fell the trees ahead,
    others tumble the rocks,
While others cut and smooth the flagstones with iron tools.
Then the masons,
    with heated sand that is mixed with volcanic tufa,
Put this down as a base on which the flagstones are laid.
And still others
    go ahead to drain the pools
Bridging those thirsty streams that lie ahead.

A Punic tombstone from Carthage with the symbol, an upraised hand, of the goddess Tanit

"Carthage must be blotted out."

It was inevitable that Rome and Carthage would one day come to war. In 264 B.C. Rome was thought to be, by Carthage, a kind of upstart. Who was Rome? But then, who or what was Carthage?

In 264 B.C. Carthage was the most powerful trading nation of the Mediterranean world. It had been settled by a tribe of Phoenicians, one of the earliest of seafaring peoples, whose original home was at Tyre, now called Sur, in Lebanon. It is said that a Phoenician called Cadmus invented the alphabet, which may well be true. While they did *not* invent the ship, they developed it—large ships with sails and oars that could and did move distantly out into the Atlantic.

In the ninth century B.C., they put their ships into shore at a place which they later called Karthadshat (Carthage), in North Africa. It had a protected bay and near it was a large lake. It was separated from Italy and Sicily at the narrow

The harbor of Carthage as it looks today. The hourglass-shaped lagoon, once rectangular, held the commercial fleet; the circular harbor was the military harbor.

waist of the Mediterranean Sea. On a clear day on a high mountain, one could see Sicily. And on a day as clear as crystal, Italy itself. Since 600 B.C., the people of Carthage had ruled the world of trade. They settled parts of the islands of Sicily and Sardinia and went on to Spain. Trade was their real interest, and they traveled far and wide to establish trading colonies.

Hanno, one of their generals, sailed in 547 B.C. through the Strait of Gibraltar into the forbidding sea. He turned his ships southward, and for the first time Mediterraneans saw a new Africa—the Africa of huge animals and immense jungles. To protect their fleet of trading vessels, the Carthaginians had to create a war fleet. And, to protect both, they built a port-fortress at Carthage—the greatest defense harbor that man, up to that time, had built.

First they built a wall. Starting at the sea on the rock-bound shore, it extended inland for about twenty-two miles and was one hundred feet high. The walls were thirty-three feet thick, with tall fighting towers every six hundred feet. On the lower levels were stalls for four thousand horses and for elephants. There, too, were barracks for their troops. Inside of the walls were living quarters, tall apartment houses for the simple man, villas for the rich.

Then they built a large artificial harbor. Back of the break-water that faced and held off the open sea was the entrance to the commercial harbor. The entrance was narrow, less than seventy feet wide. A great iron chain made of links, each one of which weighed as much as a man, was lowered to allow the passage of a vessel. After passing the fortresses on either side, ships went into a large rectangular harbor, large enough, said those who saw it, to shelter four hundred of their ships. Back of this was the military harbor. In the center was an island with the admiral's tower. It rose six stories high and from it the admiral could see any ship arriving and departing. Sicily, sixty miles away, could be clearly seen. And the admiral could look down and personally direct the ships that were berthed in the circular arcade. It could hold two hundred warships of the type called *trireme*, long, narrow ships with three banks of oars and a single lateen sail. In each warship were sixty trained oarsmen who could row as one.

Carthage was strong, rich, and aggressive. She had treaties with Rome before 350 B.C. When a Roman delegation came to trade for the famous hard wheat grown in the hinterlands of Carthage, they were scorned, since they wanted to pay less than the Carthaginians asked. The head of state of Carthage pointed to the blue sea that lapped at the great harbor, and said:

"You Romans could not even wash your hands in this sea without our permission."

The Romans never forgot this. They disliked the sea and called it "a pasture for fools." However, they soon grew to understand that if they were to defeat the Carthaginians they would have to have a navy.

In 258 B.C. the Romans found a warship of Carthage on the beach. Using this derelict ship as a model, the Romans built a fleet of one hundred ships. Instead of three banks of oars they put in five. They called these ships *quinqueremes*.

It was off the shores of Sicily that the First Punic War began in 264 B.C. These were to be the most extended wars the world, up to then, had ever known. They spread to Sardinia, Spain, and Italy and ended in Africa. They took most of Rome's energy for over a century, and work on the stone-laid roads came to a halt. The first war lasted for twenty-three years. The war consumed men and ships in such vast numbers that the first war ended in mutual exhaustion.

The Second Punic War began in Spain (Hispania). Han-

A Roman road in Palermo, Sicily, running close to the Tyrrhenian Sea

nibal, one of the greatest generals in history, was then only twenty-nine years old. He had been reared in Spain. He clearly saw that the only way to defeat the Romans was to conquer Rome itself. Of all people, he came nearest to destroying it.

In 218 B.C. he set off toward Rome with a large army, and a troop of thirty-seven war elephants. He marched from Spain into France and crossed the Alps during an early September snow. Although the Gauls had often passed over the Alps to attack the Roman settlers in the Po Valley, Hannibal made the first crossing of it with a large army. He arrived in Italy with twenty thousand men, six thousand cavalry and one elephant.

For fifteen years, between 218 and 203 B.C., Hannibal defeated every Roman legion sent after him. He ravaged the

Italian lands, captured cities, destroyed Roman towns and bridges. He was never defeated. The loss of Roman lives was awesome. The Roman army was a citizen army, and this meant that men who worked their farms or who constructed roads and bridges were among the dead.

Rome built no new roads during the war with Hannibal. However, she had to keep up the roads already begun so that troops might use them, so that the legions could move rapidly from one place to another. Roads had to be maintained in order that the produce of the farms—wheat and barley, pigs and cattle—could be brought to the markets.

The Romans had built numerous short roads coming out of Rome, and one of the most important of the northbound roads was the Via Flaminia. It had been first laid down in 264 B.C. The engineers laid the roadbed of the Flaminian Way across fertile lands. Fifty miles from the capital it entered the city of Narni (Narnia). Loftily placed, it was a natural fortress. They did not make an attempt to bridge the deep valley, a task that was left to the Emperor Augustus

Relief of a Punic-trained elephant, covered in mail, like those used by Hannibal when he crossed the Alps into Italy in 218 B.C.

The old Via Flaminia, the great northern road out of Rome,
seen today beside the modern road about ten miles from Rome

at a later date. The Flaminian Way was pushed rapidly, and it reached the town of Spoleto (Spoletium) in 220 B.C. The Romans had reason to be sorry for this because two years later Hannibal marched along the newly made road to attack Rome.

The market at the Milvian Bridge in Rome, from which the Via Flaminia led north, was a lively area. It was famed for its roast pork (and still is). Huge pigs were deboned, the head and feet trussed up, and then roasted after being generously garnished with salt, pepper, and rosemary leaves. It was here that Nero used to go in his youth, dressed as a plebeian and taking great joy in his own merry pranks.

The Second Punic War was entering its thirteenth year on Italian soil in 205 B.C., and there seemed to be no end to it. One Roman legion after another had been defeated. Hannibal believed that his victories would cause the tribes and cities of Italy to fall away from Rome. But nearly all remained loyal to Rome. Hannibal could not get reinforcements, since Roman ships held the sea. The Romans could not defeat him, and he could not take Rome.

By the year 204 B.C. it became the turn of Cornelius Scipio to take a strong hand in the war with Carthage. He had been only twenty-six when he made his fame as a commander in Spain. His father, of the same name, had been killed in Spain in those unending wars with the Carthaginians. His fame grew to such lengths that he was brought back from Spain to Rome, where he was elected consul.

The first tunnel of the Furlo Pass on the Via Flaminia. The tunnel is thirty feet long and was probably built by Gaius Flaminius in 220 B.C.

Ruins of the Baths of Antoninus close to the harbor of Carthage. They were built in the second century to beautify the new Roman Carthage.

Cornelius Scipio had many of the same qualities that would mark Julius Caesar as an unusual man. He had enthusiasm, he inspired his men with confidence, and to each enterprise that he undertook he gave intense preparation.

Rome had lost 500,000 men in the last twenty-five years of battle. Hannibal had ruined Italian lands and no general had defeated him. What could Scipio do to defeat Hannibal?

"Give me leave to take my Roman legions to attack Carthage."

It was a bold move, but leave was given and in the spring of 204 B.C., Scipio, with an army of 25,000 men, landed near Carthage. This was the beginning of real Roman influence in that area. Rome was to remain in Africa for centuries. She was to build hundreds of beautiful cities, cross North Africa with roads, and make the desert bloom as never before—or since.

But first Carthage had to be defeated. Scipio landed near Carthage, and the people of Carthage sent off a swift sailing ship to Italy to advise Hannibal to return.

In the year 203 B.C. he prepared for his return to Carthage. Hannibal knew that his opportunity was lost.

"The gods gave me the chance to take Rome, but I had not the will. Now it is too late. The gods give no second opportunities."

He had gathered his men for their winter quarters in the southern part of Italy, at the place now called Crotone, and there he waited for the ships. They came in their endless parade, and while waiting he wrote his paean of victory and then had the words cast in a bronze plaque. Proud to the end, he told of all his victories over the Romans. He had the tablet attached to the wall of the Greek Temple of Hera at Crotone. Then he sailed.

The next year, 202 B.C., the Roman and Carthaginian armies met on Carthage's land. The armies were about equal in size and experience, and they were led by two of the finest generals of their time. But Scipio had superiority in horsemen. Hannibal's war elephants led the charge. The Roman army divided and let the elephants plow harmlessly to the rear. Then the well-trained legions closed in battle, and their horsemen attacked the flanks of Hannibal's army. The Carthaginian army broke and Hannibal escaped to Carthage.

For the victories that Scipio won over Hannibal he took the surname of Africanus, said to have been the name of Hannibal's mother. (After Carthage was destroyed in 146 B.C., the territory that had once been hers became the Roman province of Africa.)

The terms of Roman peace at the end of the Second Punic War were harsh: Carthage must give up all her warships and war elephants; it must yield up all African land outside Car-

The remains of ancient Carthage: a cemetery near Byrsa Hill with the distinctive Punic gravestones, under each a bowl of cremated bones.

thage itself; silver was to be paid to Rome—ten thousand talents, or eighty million dollars, over a period of fifty years.

And yet, with all this imposed upon her, Carthage again grew strong. Carthage complained to the Roman Senate about the way she had been bound by the treaty, and demanded that a commission be sent out from Rome to see for itself. The committee was led by a senator named Cato. What he saw he did not like. Rome had fought Carthage for over one hundred years and Carthage was growing strong again. After that, in the Senate, no matter what the argument, Cato would end each speech:

". . . for the rest it is my opinion that CARTHAGE MUST BE DESTROYED."

In 153 B.C. Cato was eighty-one years old. He had served in the wars in Spain, he had been wounded several times in the wars against Hannibal in Italy, and the memory of all this was very much alive in the old senator. So at the end of every debate in the Senate, no matter how far removed was the subject of the debate from Carthage, he said, very firmly:

". . . in my opinion Carthage must be blotted out."

In 146 B.C., Cato had his wish.

If a people desires war it can always create its own reasons, and Rome asked things of Carthage that Carthage could not give. And this was enough. The Romans brought up a huge army and navy. The siege went on for three years. In the end Carthage was, as Cato had wished, "blotted out."

When Scipio Africanus Minor, its Roman conqueror, adopted grandson of Africanus who had defeated Hannibal, looked over the ruins of the city, its proud buildings tumbled, its magnificent harbor a smoking ruin, he said to his secretary, Polybius, who took down all of these events in writing, "This is a glorious moment for Rome. Yet I am seized with fear and foreboding that someday the same fate will befall Rome, my own city."

IV

Remains of a fortified Roman farm in the Libyan desert in North Africa

Africa, "That wilderness of elephants"

After the fall of Carthage, Rome did not, as was her usual practice, immediately send over her engineers to begin the system of roads she was later to build in North Africa. The Senate of Rome put a solemn curse on Carthage. It must be utterly destroyed. The ground be salted. On pain of death no one was to rebuild the city. The Romans merely took control of the lands that were Carthage's and also established the protected state of Numidia.

Ivory, gold, wood, precious stones, animals, slaves from this land had enriched Carthage, but Africa at first bewildered the Romans. The legions that had been sent out to explore Africa had come back with strange reports. Back of the coast were lands where wheat was raised, but it was haunted by wild animals. There were high mountains that were snow-covered in winter, then there was a vast nothing of sand, and at rare intervals oases of date palms. There were

57

A pre-Roman mausoleum in Carthage. It was built in the third century B.C. *to hold the remains of Ateban, son of Iepmatatah, son of Paln, chief of the Numidians.*

wild tribes who attacked; lions and leopards and vast herds of trumpeting elephants.

For a long time the Romans did not realize the extent of their prize. Poets made fun of the land, so dearly won with Roman blood; "Africa, that arid nurse of lions," said one, and another: "Africa, that wilderness of elephants." So Rome turned its back on the land and let Africa settle back to its own native ways, under her watchful eye, of course. There it lay for one hundred years.

Julius Caesar changed this. In order to make himself the ruler of Rome he had to fight those Romans who opposed him. Everywhere they went he followed — Italy, Greece, Spain, Egypt, and finally Africa. At the Battle of Thapsus, on the shore of the Mediterranean Sea in 46 B.C., in what is

now Tunisia, he finally defeated the last of his foes and said:
"I take possession of thee, O Africa."

As Carthage was near to his own battlefield, he visited it.
With his own eyes he saw the ruined palaces and temples,
and the once great harbor still filled with broken ships and
tumbled wharves. It distressed him much. That night, he
wrote, he had a dream; a divinity had appeared to him and
said: "Rebuild Carthage."

Julius Caesar began to lay down his plans for the taking
over of North Africa. First, the city of Rome, now half a
million, needed wheat. Africa was famous for its hard wheat
and Carthage was only two days' sail from the port of Ostia.
It was too rich a land to share with the natives. But then
came the Ides of March in 44 B.C. and Julius Caesar was
murdered.

Once Rome decided to undertake anything, she went about
it in a very efficient manner. The next ruler, Octavian, created
in 40 B.C. a Roman legion to command North Africa. It was
later called the Legio III Augusta. Their orders: to organize
the three million square miles of the coast and desert of
North Africa. The Roman soldier was trained to level forests,
lay down roads, build bridges, and aid in planning a city.
Rome sent out its best engineers and its best architects.
Many of the new cities were set upon cities that had already
been built by Carthage. If those cities fitted into Roman
plans, they were used; if not, they were destroyed and the
stones used to make a new city. If the new city had not the
proper roads, they were built. If an old road could be used
and remade, it was done; if not, a new road was put down.

The natives of the country, the Berbers, used to the suffo-
cating heat, were used as laborers. Prisoners of war were set
to work, and, when these were not enough, slaves.

By 19 B.C. enough roads and cities had been constructed

Tunisian landscape: the grove of olive trees camouflages a large Roman city; beyond are wheat fields and terraced hills planted with fir trees.

to receive the first three thousand colonists sent out by the Emperor Augustus. Roman soldiers who had been discharged from the army after twenty years of service now came in droves to Africa. They were given as much land as they could plow, and animals were provided by the state. Loans at small rates of interest were given to them to begin to colonize Africa. These were the *coloni*. They could not leave their farms without permission. They then began to plow their lands and plant the famous hard wheat of Africa. At first they used bullocks, but when camels began to come in from the Far East, they learned to hitch these one-humped dromedaries to their wooden plows.

The valleys of North Africa, in those countries now known as Algeria and Tunisia, have flatlands that lie between the mountains. There is only a short rainy season, and in this time the farmer must plant his wheat. Then comes the torrid period. The wheat grows and ripens very slowly without water, but if the elements are kind, the farmer can harvest a good crop of hard wheat.

Within fifty years wheat from Africa was pouring into Rome. Three thousand grain ships—large, stout, widely built—sailed between Africa and Ostia loaded with hard wheat for Rome. If the wind was right it was only a forty-eight-hour sail. From Ostia the wheat ships were then towed up the seventeen miles to Rome itself, pulled up by mules that walked the bank of the river. Wheat was still given to the people of Rome. In time Africa Proconsularis was sending over ten million bushels of wheat yearly to Rome. If the grain ships were delayed, the common people would riot for

The famous hard wheat of Tunisia, which matures slowly under the dry heat of the African sun.

*An ancient Roman road out of Dougga (Thugga) in Tunisia.
From here, it joins the Roman road from Carthage to Tebessa, Algeria.*

their wheat dole. Rome soon realized Africa's importance. "Whoever held Africa held Rome."

And so the extensive road-building program began. As it rained only a few days out of the year, the Roman engineers soon found that they need not make the foundations for their roads as deep as in Italy. Most of the African land, when it is not soil or sand, is limestone or sandstone. The engineers dug through the surface until they struck solid rock, and then laid the roadbed on top of it. Roads were built higher in the center so that the water could run off. The builders found that as the earth hardened quickly after a rainfall, almost as hard as stone itself, they did not have to pave it. That saved time and money. Only in the cities did they lay down stone pavements.

Roman road leading into Sbeitla (Sufetula) in Tunisia. The gleaming white rectangular stones were cut to bring them flush with the curbing.

The Roman streets and roads were paved with huge stones weighing as much as two hundred pounds and shaped on several sides. The African streets were paved with rectangular stones. Still, whether it was Rome or Africa, the streets were laid down over carefully worked-out drains that carried away the rain water. This was caught up and held in cisterns.

Roman cities sprang up all over North Africa between the years 40 B.C. and A.D. 100. These were not small rustic villages; they were cities. At the entrance to each city the people erected a handsomely carved arch. Usually this was put up to honor an emperor. As soon as one entered upon the paved streets, there would be a public toilet with constantly running water. There were public baths, with hot and cold water. The rooms, in cold weather, were heated indirectly; under the

One of the underground rooms in a palace in Bulla Reggia in Tunisia.
Because of the heat, sometimes 120 degrees in the shade in the summer,
the Roman patricians built part of their houses below ground. It was
20 degrees cooler in the "under-palace" during the hot season.

floor and behind the walls of the baths hollow tiles carried
warm air. If one had the money, there were private baths
where libraries were available. Books of famous Greek and
Roman authors could be read before and after the bath. In

almost every African city with over fifty thousand inhabitants there was a theater. Actors came from Greece and Rome. There was a circus where chariot races were held. In a city called Thysdrus, now El Djem, the Romans built a colosseum so gigantic that it could seat over thirty thousand people at one time; it is only a few feet smaller in size than the great one in Rome. It still stands today and it shows the great concern that Rome had for the entertainment of its people.

In time, the villas of the rich were the most splendid outside of Rome. The floors were paved in mosaics of different colored stones. In the bathroom, tile dolphins swam about with sea nymphs, while various kinds of fish moved about in a stone mimicry of nature.

It is believed that the climate of North Africa then was not much different from what it is today. As the inner land is

The remains of the Roman amphitheater, designed to seat 30,000 people, at El Djem in Tunisia. It was built by Gordian.

mountainous, the rain that fell flowed down toward the sea. At the coast the water penetrated the ground and made the land fertile. Yet not all the coast was verdured. There were vast spaces where the desert came down to the sea, and sand dunes were always shifting back and forth.

It took some time for the Romans to master a way to build a road along the shore of North Africa. Most of the great cities were built by the sea and each had its own port but no road to unite one with another.

In A.D. 98 the Emperor Nerva ordered the legion to begin a road that would connect all the cities of Carthage with the cities to the east. Nerva, when he became emperor in A.D. 96, was then over sixty years old. He did not have the strength to visit Africa personally, so he adopted, as was a Roman custom, a worthy younger man. Nerva adopted a young senator named Trajan as his son and his heir. Trajan was born in Roman Spain at Italica. He was destined to be one of the greatest emperors Rome ever had. He also built more roads than any other prince before or after him. The old emperor, Nerva, was on his deathbed in A.D. 98 when the great North African coastal road was begun. It became the duty of Trajan to see it completed. He went to Africa in A.D. 113 to see that it was done.

The Via Nerva, named after the late emperor, passed from that part of the territory of Carthage later called Byzacium into Tripoli. This area got its name from the three great coastal cities, Sabrata, Oea, and Leptis Magna (*tri*, three, and *poli*, cities). The Roman legions, with their roadworkers, had to level the sand dunes. They had to remove tough grass and take out twisted tree stumps in order to find a good base for their road. Even as they do today, the workers had to live in tents. Water and food had to be brought to them. As all work was done by hand, it was a laborious business. Yet

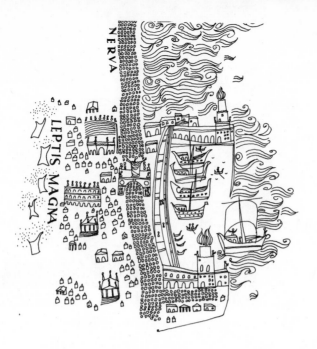

in time they conquered the sand and the road entered the first city.

Sabrata, now called Sabratha, had been a pre-Roman city, and the Romans rebuilt it. It was given a harbor and paved streets, and in time people built their houses within the city. Even today, after two thousand years, one can see how luxurious it once was.

In the center of Sabratha, to which the coastal road led, was the forum. It was beautifully paved in white limestone. At one end was the temple. Wagons could roll up to the forum with supplies. Around it were shops and taverns. Here people gathered for information, for gossip, to vote, or to exchange ideas. Here business was conducted. The remains of a large theater, built near the sea, give an idea of the wealth of the city.

The road went on fifty miles east to the next of the three cities, Oea. Like the others it was an ancient trading center. The Romans rebuilt it. While there is not much left of ancient Oea today (it is now the thriving port of Tripoli) there is a large triumphal arch set up to the glory of Marcus Aurelius.

The two-wheeled oxcart was used for heavy goods; this fragment from North Africa shows such a wagon carrying an oxhide of wine.

It was under this arch that the coastal road entered the city.

Trade is the lifeblood of nations. The goods they produce must be traded for others they do not produce. Africa sent olive oil, hard wheat, and wild animals to Rome. The need for animals—lions, leopards, hyenas, bears, wolves, elephants, ostriches—was so great that Oea had thousands of people engaged in trapping animals. Five thousand animals were killed in a single week at the opening of the great Colosseum in Rome. There were hundreds of such colosseums all over the Roman world. For every lion that arrived in Rome alive, perhaps three had died en route. The farmer in Africa was happy to trap the animals, for many of them trampled down his wheat or ate the leaves off his trees. Lions and other meat-eating animals killed his cows and pigs. So over the coastal road large solid-wheeled carts brought cages filled with animals. Their destiny: death in the Colosseum.

As the coastal road crawled on its way eastward toward Egypt, it came from time to time to oases filled with date palms. This was another food for the Roman market. Where there was an oasis there was water, and at these points the soldier-builder of the road did not have to dig wells. Along the road water had to be stored every twenty miles for the traveler's use. This was done either by digging a deep well or catching water off a roof and storing it in a cement cistern.

On the way toward Egypt the Via Nerva next passed through Leptis Magna, modern Lebda, the largest city on the coast. Around it in the hinterland were planted, it is said, more than two million olive trees. It is fully possible, because Julius Caesar, in 46 B.C., made that city pay a tax of three million measures of pressed oil every year to Rome. The olive oil from Africa was coarse and heavy, so it was used for lamps and for the bath. It was the custom at the time to scrape the skin with a metal spatula and rub olive oil on the body before bathing.

The amphitheater at Leptis Magna, one of the Roman African coastal cities

No one knows how large the city was, because much of it is still buried under sand. But it had a large circus, among the largest known, an immense theater, and baths that were thought to rival those of Rome. Its buildings were most ornate. Above all there was the artificial harbor. If much of it did not still exist, it would be difficult to accept descriptions of it.

Leptis Magna had a small natural harbor, which the Romans transformed into an immense artificial harbor facing the open sea. A mole made of massive stones was built as a breakwater. The inner harbor was a mile in circumference. On both sides were massive lighthouses, square towers, parts of which still stand. To the left was a temple, then the customhouse, and all around it the storerooms of merchants. All this was built on a vast scale. From it one can form an idea of how modern were the ideas of the Romans. And how practical. An ancient writer remembered seeing ". . . quantities of wheat, barley, wine, oil, and other fruits of the earth" stacked for shipment to Rome.

In Africa, too, the Roman legions had to worry about rivers. Each river, or wadi, no matter how small or dry in the hot months, had to be bridged. When rain falls the wadis suddenly become raging torrents of water. The soldier-engineers went into the interior, and across the wadis they built dams or barrages. Every mile or so, or even closer, they built a stone dam to break the force of the water. These were put up so that the water would not eat away the banks, wash away roads, or sweep away trees. They are found far back in the interior of these barren lands. After roads, bridges, and dams, the legions had to worry about protection for the Roman cities.

As is natural, the natives were not overjoyed when the Romans moved in. When the Carthaginians ruled the land,

A Roman bridge, built in the second century, spanning a small brook in Tunisia. The bed of the brook was paved with large stones so that the rush of water would not wear away the foundation.

they left the natives very much to themselves. When the Romans arrived they began to organize their lives. The natives brought down ivory, gold, ebony, animal skins, ostrich feathers, rare stones, a peculiar stone called the carbuncle, and finally slaves.

A great desert tribe, the Garamantes, was the largest and most feared. They hunted men as they did animals and brought down black men from the Sudan, ". . . a strange, childlike people," wrote a Roman, "who never killed cattle but raised them as objects of homely affection." Many people were traders in men. The Greeks took part in it and called it "the silent trade." Before slaves were sent to Rome, each had a scroll put around his neck, the *titulus*. It gave the birthplace, age, and health of each.

These Fezzan tribes believed that when Carthage fell they would be able to take over the coast trade. In A.D. 69 the

The three temples of Sbeitla, deep in the interior of Tunisia in an area famous for its olive trees.

citizens of Leptis "trembled," said a Roman historian, "at the approach of the Garamantes." For three months they had the city under siege, and they were only routed when the Legio III Augusta arrived. The Romans pursued them into the desert, one thousand miles into the utter nothing.

After that the Romans built a series of fortified farms and outposts to hold the natives in check. This had to be done before they could build their road toward Egypt.

The Via Nerva-Traiana extended one thousand and four miles in length. It began at the borders of Carthage at the Roman city of Tacape, now called Gabès, and moved through the desert and the oases; sand and quicksand did not stop it. As wide as twenty feet, built so that the center part was highest, the road kept its appointed way. Where once the Greeks had settled, in Cyrenaica, the Akhdar Mountains come close to the sea. There the Romans cut out the rock so that the road might be kept in a straight line. There was a Roman station at Paraetonium, known today as Mersa Matrûh and famous during the World War II desert campaign. From here

Ancient Dougga, famed for splendid buildings, aqueduct, and theater.

the road entered Egypt. The final goal and end of the road was at Alexandria.

Alexandria was founded by Alexander the Great in 332 B.C. Before his time the city was a sleepy little fishing village at the place where the most westerly branch of the Nile empties into the sea. Alexander commanded that a city be built. What had been the lair of pirates and the home of the hippopotami that swam in fetid Nile waters was now a famed city and port.

Via Nerva-Traiana reached Egypt after A.D. 113. Alexandria had long since become part of Rome. It had had a trade treaty with Rome as early as 273 B.C. In 30 B.C., Egypt became a Roman possession.

Since the Nile River served as a river road, it was not necessary for the Romans to build a network of land roads in Egypt. But roads they built. One went up the west side of the Nile, three hundred miles to the First Cataract. Three roads started out of Memphis, an ancient city located on the west bank of the Nile some distance from the sea. One road went east along the shore of the Mediterranean toward Palestine. Another went east across the sands and rocks of Arabia, passing north of Mount Sinai, where Moses is said to have gotten the tablets of the law from the hand of God. And the last road, built in Egypt by the Emperor Trajan, went over the high, arid mountains that lie between the Nile and the Red Sea.

These joined the thousand-mile-long desert road, which came to an end at the city of Alexandria, in the very shadow of the greatest lighthouse in the world. Where the Romans placed their last milestone, marking the end of the Roman desert road, there, offshore, stood the Pharos of Alexandria.

The lighthouse was over 400 feet in height (only about 100 feet less than that of the Washington Monument). It was

ALEXANDRIA

built in three sections, and so immense that it contained fifty rooms. A stairway led to the top, where a huge fire was kept going night and day; it was one of the Seven Wonders of the World. For fifteen hundred years it guided ships and mariners in these uncertain seas. Alexander decreed that his name, and his alone, should be on the Pharos, but the builder, a crafty Greek, carved an inscription on the walls and covered it over with plaster. In time the plaster fell off and it could be read:

"This Pharos was built by Sostratus, son of Dexiphanes, on behalf of all Mariners to the savior gods."

It endured until it was destroyed by an earthquake, about A.D. 1300. In A.D. 1154 an Arab geographer, the Spanish Moor al-Idrisi, companion to Roger of Normandy, reported:

". . . we noticed the lighthouse. It has not its like in the world . . . it is built of excellent stone and instead of cement the stones are joined together with molten lead. The distance from the lighthouse to the city is one mile by water.

"One climbs to the summit by a broad staircase built into the interior . . . until the lighthouse rises and until at last one reaches the top. There, at the pinnacle, is the beacon. It is kept lit night and day for sailors during the entire sailing season. Mariners know the fire beacon and direct their ships accordingly. It is visible one hundred miles away. At night it looks like a brilliant star . . ."

The Romans brought their land road across the desert to Alexandria to tie up with the roads of the Middle East.

V

Ruins at Jerash in Jordan, one of the great Roman caravan cities

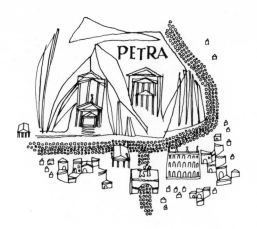

The Roads to the Spiceries

The Romans had been in that part of the world they called Hither Asia as early as 200 B.C. Roman merchants lived there by treaty. The first Roman foothold in the Middle East was for peaceful trade.

For centuries the simple Roman had lived on porridge, though sometimes he might afford "plain roast Roman pork." Fish was eaten only by those who lived near the sea. Ice and cold storage rooms were not used until A.D. 350, so only that which could be eaten within two days could be kept in the house. The state had set up a sort of standard of living for all the people. Wheat was given free, the price of salt was regulated. Circuses and theaters, chariot races and games were arranged for the people. If food was not equally distributed, the people rioted. The things that people spoke about in the streets influenced the political powers in Rome.

After the final victory in the Punic Wars, Rome was unified. It was strong and aggressive and its numbers grew and its wealth multiplied. Trading stations were set up throughout the Roman Empire, and Roman businessmen traded for the luxuries now wanted. It was not simple. In Hither Asia were lands of ancient culture. Many city states had grown up, prospered, and died here long before the Romans had even appeared. It was a land of intense rivalry. Goods that the Romans had ordered were often lost because of the bad roads or road robbers. In 129 B.C. a Roman official, M.' Aquillius, began to build the first of the Roman roads in the land now called Turkey; one day it would become a road system. To protect her trade, Rome first took over Antioch, and by 64 B.C. all Syria. In the year 3 B.C., under the direct orders of Augustus, a road was built along the rugged coast of Turkey. It was named the Via Sebaste and went from Ephesus to Tarsus.

The great architect-general Agrippa, whose name still adorns the Pantheon in Rome, had been sent out by Augustus to Romanize the ancient city of Antioch, onetime capital of the Seleucid kings. Agrippa built beautiful colonnaded streets. The city was walled, and the roads were laid out in Roman style, eighteen feet wide with tightly fitting stones, so well constructed that the roads are still in use.

With each passing decade and with each new emperor the Romans expanded in Hither Asia. In the time of Vespasian, Jerash was rebuilt. By A.D. 70 the city was ready to receive the caravans from the Red Sea, laden with trade goods. A large hippodrome stood outside the city walls. The caravans entered the south gate, passed the forum and into the market. Jerash was one of the key cities on the caravan route. Palmyra, Jerash, and Petra were the three important caravan cities. The Emperor Trajan, in A.D. 106, ordered a magnificent series of roads to be built to reach Jerash, and as its wealth grew, old buildings were torn down and others rebuilt. It was at its greatest when the people of Jerash, at their expense, built

a triumphal arch for the arrival of the Emperor Hadrian in
A.D. 130.

Trajan, the greatest builder of roads Rome ever had, improved the existing roads all over Hither Asia. He called
over two legions: the Legio III Cyrenaica guarded the north,
the Legio VIII Hispania, drawn from his own Spain, guarded
the south.

They kept the Pax Romana, or Roman Peace. They taught
the people how to build roads and how to put up bridges.
They erected guard stations and signal towers. Over the land
came something the people had not known for centuries—
security. With security came growth and freedom, trade and
movement. Desert posts, forts, and checkpoints were put up
to control the unruly tribesmen; swift Roman justice was
meted out to those who broke the Pax Romana. In that
atmosphere, the arts of peace, of which road building was
one, flourished.

The great Via Traiana, ordered, built, and most of it personally financed by Trajan, ran the whole length of the desert
land from Damascus to Aqaba, the port of the Red Sea
route. It extended for four hundred miles, and to the north
ran parallel to the river Jordan and the Dead Sea. Trajan
appointed a well-known builder of roads, Claudius Severus,
to be his legate and overseer of the southern sections of the
road. At the Wadi Musa, the road followed a deep canyon
to the famous city of Petra. Petra belonged once to the
Nabataean kingdom. It is these people who began the famous
rock city; its buildings, of the most beautiful classical style,
were hewn out of the varicolored limestone.

The Romans took over Petra in A.D. 106 to protect the
caravans that went through these canyons. Whoever controlled Petra controlled the caravan route. Petra was rede-
signed on Roman lines; streets, fountains, theaters, all went

The Roman road to Petra, whose temples were cut into the pink limestone cliffs, was flanked by columns.

up in the usual fashion. The ancient buildings of the Nabataeans they left alone.

Seventy Roman miles from Petra, the Via Traiana entered the port of Aqaba. There are no archaeological remains here, only memory and bits of history. Aqaba provided the shortest route to the Middle East; caravans of ships sailed from Bombay into the Arabian Sea, avoiding the pirates if they could at the narrows of the Gulf of Aden. Then, with the trade winds, they sailed north on the Red Sea to the port of Aqaba. It was the roadhead for the desert caravans.

The Romans had a passion for pepper. It gave food a bounce. It was light and easily transportable. Loaded onto camels, it was brought four hundred miles over Trajan's Way, put on ships at the ports of Lebanon and then sent to Ostia, the port of Rome. The filling of the pepper barns beside the Tiber was one of the primary functions of trade. So important was pepper that when the Goths appeared before the gates of Rome in A.D. 408 they demanded three thousand pounds of pepper before they would treat with the Romans.

Cinnamon, "the gift of kings," arrived at Aqaba curled up in long, pencil-shaped sticks. Cloves, called "little nails" because the head of a clove looked like a Roman nail, made its way from Ceylon. Nutmeg and its covering, mace, came from Malaya. Gingerroot, which grew in the wild parts of India, was easily packed and could withstand the many days of the long haul. These spices were best for trade; cheap at the source, they were dear at the market. Spices were light and easily transportable. Pliny, the great Roman naturalist, who was so curious about nature that he walked too near Vesuvius during its eruption and died of asphyxia, said about the spice trade: "They sold at the market of Rome for a hundred times their original price."

"Bring us slaves and bring us ivory," was the demand of the rich in Rome. Both arrived at Aqaba. The whole ancient world, not alone Rome, dealt in slavery; conquered peoples, people who could not pay their debts, people who sold themselves into slavery, and others uprooted from their homes, all were brought into the slave markets.

And ivory—Romans had a passion for it. Judges sat on seats plaited with ivory. The seats and the benches of the Roman Senate were of ivory. One Roman emperor had his horses eat from ivory mangers. Ivory was delicate in color with the feel of a water lily. It was never cold nor dead. It grew more beautiful with age. It was strong and elastic and could be easily and deeply cut. Roman jewelers loved to inlay ivory with gold or turquoise.

Pearls came from the coasts of India, carried by traders and guarded by soldiers. Pearls relate themselves to flesh, and Roman women were proud when their skin gave the pearls sheen and sweetness. The best pearls came from Ceylon.

"I swear before the gods," said a returning trader, "that the bottom of the sea seems to be covered with them. There is no place in the world where more pearls are found."

And with pearls from India came diamonds. These were found in the gravel of river beds. That "invincible stone," they said of it because it could not be cut. The Romans called it by its Greek name *adamas*, meaning invulnerable. Kings who went to war placed them on their breastplates near to their hearts so that they would not be killed. The diamond was thought to be frozen water.

Emeralds came from India as well as from Egypt. And there were all the rainbow jewels destined for Rome: jade and jasper, agate and onyx, beryl and sapphire, "the most like heaven in fair weather and clear, most apt to fit the fingers of kings."

All these products of trade were luxury items. They were light and easily transportable; cheap at the source, and worth a fortune in Rome.

There were other trade items: linen and cotton, bananas and sugar cane. The banana, which is really a grass, was first developed in India. Only the traders knew of it and ate it. Bananas were bulky to ship, the passage to Rome too long to have them arrive eatable. Sugar cane was known to the Romans, but honey was the sweetener. Linens and cottons were, of course, known; mummies had been wrapped in linen, it could be woven almost as thin as silk.

The Indians cultivated cotton trees, and this cotton was known as "tree wool." In the Nile they grew a bush cotton, the long-staple cotton beloved by the weavers of cloth. They made gauzy tissues of cotton of a thinness like a veil of mist, "there is a cloth a yard wide and twenty yards long that can be passed through a finger ring."

At the port of Aqaba, merchants had offices where the imports were received and duties paid. The merchants waited to load the camel caravans until there was a large enough shipment—caravans numbered as many as five hundred camels. If the cargo was very precious, a company of the Roman legion, commanded by a centurion, was sent along to protect it. The camel made the caravan possible.

It is said that the first camel the Romans saw was in 46 B.C., when Julius Caesar, at the Battle of Thapsus, in North Africa, captured twenty-seven of them as part of his war booty. But as Romans had been in Hither Asia since 200 B.C., it seems certain that they knew of this strange beast before.

But they seem never to have been curious about it. It is never seen on the early monuments of Egypt, it did not come to Africa until late in history. Camels were used during the wars of the Persians and Greeks and "the reason," said a Greek, "of putting the camels face to face with the horses of the enemy is that horses fear camels and can endure neither the sight nor the smell of them."

The camel came from Asia. There are two kinds: a two-humped camel, the Bactrian, which provides a natural saddle between the humps, and a single-humped camel, the dromedary. The name camel comes from the Arabic *jamal*. Wild camels are unknown. They live with man. Alive or dead, they contain in their bodies almost all that a desert traveler must have. Their milk is drunk, their dung is used for firewood, their flesh can be eaten. The hair of the camel is soft and can be woven into cloth or into tough weavings for the Arabs' "black tents." They can carry a load of five hundred pounds twenty-five miles a day. They can live ten days without drinking water. Their nostrils have trap doors to keep out wind-blown sand. Their feet are like spongy foot pads and will not sink deeply into the sand. They can outrun a horse and can carry eight times more than a man can carry and four times that of a mule. Camels live in the desert where temperatures rise to 140 degrees, or they can survive in snow-bound lands as cold as the arctic. The camel can be hitched to a wagon or to a plow. Cared for, they live long lives, but without man they cannot survive.

The important caravan routes had of course to be protected. This forced Rome to push back its frontiers to make all else secure.

East of Syria, farther east than Mesopotamia, was the vast land of the Persians, ruled then by the Parthians. Trajan pushed the Roman Empire into the lands of Parthia and brought Rome to the Persian Gulf. Trajan had set up his

Fragment of relief found in Tunisia, showing dromedary camel

headquarters at ancient Antioch. It was known as "the third city of the world" and was a favorite city of the Roman emperors. Its climate was happy and it was an important center for trade.

The legions under Trajan fought to carry the empire to the greatest limits it had ever reached. And as soon as the campaign ended, public works began. "I will," said Trajan, "use the olive wood of my sword to make war breed peace." Trajan did it by building roads and thus creating trade.

The second great caravan road of Trajan, the Via Palmyra, was built from Palmyra to Baghdad, to "the land between two rivers"—the Tigris and the Euphrates. At the river-port city of Seleucia on the Tigris, the great caravan road ended.

When the army of Trajan reached the vast plains of Mesopotamia, he had thrust Rome farther than any man before him. Yet the Parthians, in their favored land, grew strong and Rome worried that they would raid their caravans and attack their cities, their lifelines of commerce.

So "the land between two rivers" was conquered. Trajan built pontoon bridges across the Tigris and the Euphrates. As quickly as the Parthians surrendered, just as quickly did Trajan have his soldiers put them to work on the roads, to bind the land to Rome.

The emperor was aware that his roads brought nothing new to Persia. One of the earliest roads ever built had been built by the ancient Assyrians near Nineveh. Historians say that the time could have been as early as 2500 B.C. The Persians, by 600 B.C., had built some long roads. One at Susa, the capital of Darius, King of Persia, ran for nine hundred miles to what is now the city of Ankara in Turkey.

Persian cities were set between marsh and desert and the Persians were masters of travel. They bred the two-humped camel in the country of Bactria, from which it took its name,

OSTIA

and organized great camel caravans. While Rome was still a barbarous tribe on the hills above the Tiber, Persia had great trade routes. They were exact in business, and trade was their life. It was the Persians who first set up rest stations for travelers and invented the post: men riding fast-galloping horses carrying messages by relays as fast as one hundred miles a day. It is this act that so impressed the famous Greek historian Herodotus of Halicarnassus, who wrote, ". . . neither snow, nor rain, nor heat . . . stop them in their flight."

Within one year of fighting Trajan had brought his legions to the Gulf of Persia and there the conquest ended. A few years later his nephew and successor, the Emperor Hadrian, put up, at the village of Circesium, two tall towers. These marked the extreme eastern limits of the Roman Empire. He gave them in safe keeping to the god Terminus, who guarded the boundaries of the realm.

Now that the Pax Romana was secure, Trajan finished the roads. A long one was built to connect Seleucia, on the banks of the River Tigris, to Carrhae, in northern Mesopotamia. Carrhae was "where the four roads met." One went to Asia Minor, the other to Antioch, the third connected with Palmyra and then went on to Damascus and so down to Aqaba.

With this the floodgates of plenty were open to Rome. Babylonia was famed for its carpets. Apples, peaches, and nuts were cultivated. All sorts of sweets, "for sucking, for licking and chewing," poured down the caravan routes. Figs and lemons, almonds and currants came from these lands, which the Jews called the gardens of paradise. Honey came from the edge of the desert lands. Rice, a great luxury, was seen in Rome, and oil made from coconuts was imported for the making of candles and soap.

Arabia, which lay to the south, was the land of balm and incense. This was the land of aromatics, umber, and aloes, musk and rose water. Incense was needed to purify kings and gods. Arabia supplied it. There were all sorts of stones, some magical, some beautiful. A great deal of fun was made by actors on the Roman stage, poking fun at wealthy Romans who demanded so many luxuries.

No one could ever understand, for one thing, why the Romans had a passion for amber. The Greeks had called it *elektra*, "the special act of the god," and traders walked all the way from Greece to the Baltic Sea to get it. One writer said that although Roman fashion had not found any use for it, still Nero sent a knight, with a large number of men, two thousand miles to the Baltic Sea to see its place of origin.

The great Persian route opened a connection with the mysterious land of China. The chicken came from China;

and silk. Aristotle, who was the private tutor to Alexander the Great, went with him on his conquests to India. Aristotle was the first person in the Western world to mention how silk was made; "from this animal [worm] women reel off the cocoon and afterward people spin from it." The silk route came down from China into Afghanistan, and then into Syria, where the camel caravans moved it along the Roman road. In Trajan's time a pound of silk cost one pound of gold. There was a bewitchment about silk. People liked its rustle and luster. The main trade center of silk was then Palmyra at the edge of the great Arabian desert.

Later, in the reign of Marcus Aurelius, an embassy was sent to China. The Chinese called Rome Ta-Ts'in. "They traffic," the record says, "with Persia and India. The Romans are honest in trade. They have no double prices. Their kings wish to send embassies to China to trade in silk."

All the trade that flowed along the roads was protected by the Roman legions. It was funneled down to the ports on the Mediterranean Sea in the present-day country of Lebanon. There the trade goods could be carried to Rome in six days if the wind was right. Lebanon (where St. George slew the dragon) was famed throughout the world for its forests. The great mountains of Lebanon, as high as ten thousand feet, were covered with forests. There grew the erect and straight-growing cedars of Lebanon. These were a primary source of wood for the ancient Egyptians. The early Phoenicians built their ships of this cedar. And perhaps because of this source of wood they became one of the earliest seagoing people. Cedarwood from Lebanon was sent overland one thousand miles to build the great temples of Persepolis in Persia. When Solomon decided to build his temple, he asked the King of Tyre for his help to obtain wood from Lebanon.

The Temple of Jupiter at Baalbek in Lebanon, once surrounded by forty-two immense columns, was begun in reign of Antoninus Pius.

"Now therefore command them that they hew me cedar trees out of Lebanon."

Although Italy had all the wood then that a people could use, still they imported cedars. It was the fashion.

In Lebanon, at Baalbek, the Romans built the Temple of Jupiter. Its great stone columns were among the tallest in the world—sixty feet high, each weighing fifteen hundred tons. This fawn-tinged stone, quarried in Egypt, far up the Nile, was transported for three thousand miles to the Lebanon hills.

Riches poured down into the ports of the eastern Mediterranean—gold and precious stones from India, spices and silk from China, rugs from Babylonia, furs from Russia. Here there was contact with all the diverse people of a diverse world.

The Romans knew, and mostly respected, the beliefs of other people. Through contact Romans were given new ideas. Ideas bred other ideas until men learned and knew of the world beyond them. More than mere measurable things came to the market. There was thought, for example. It was easily transportable.

So the roads that the Romans sent off to the far corners of the then known world made Rome, in its time, the greatest, the most cosmopolitan city in the ancient world.

VI

On a Roman road, thirty-six miles north of Aosta (Augusta Praetoria),
Italy, leading to the Great St. Bernard Pass, the builders carved
the arch out of the solid rock.

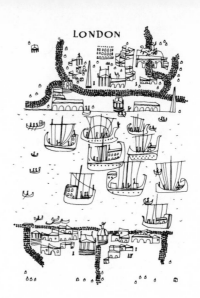

LONDON

Roads Grow Long

By A.D. 134 the Emperor Hadrian had put final bounds to the Roman Empire. For years he had given himself untiringly to the good of the empire and its people. He was, as one can see from his portraits, a man of grace and intelligence. Of his twenty-one years as Roman Emperor, more than half were spent traveling to the most distant parts of the empire.

Hadrian was born in the Roman colony of Italica, in Spain, in A.D. 76. He served Rome in many capacities, and later was adopted by Trajan as his son and heir to the empire. He was interested in art, loved Greece and its language, and collected works of art wherever his travels took him. Fortune went with him. When he toured Africa, it rained there for the first time in five years. He journeyed on to the Euphrates and there put up boundary markers.

The year A.D. 121 was spent at the borders of Germany, where, under his supervision, the *limes*, fixed line of defense, was repaired and put in military readiness. And in A.D. 122, in Britain (Britannia), he built a long wall at its narrow

95

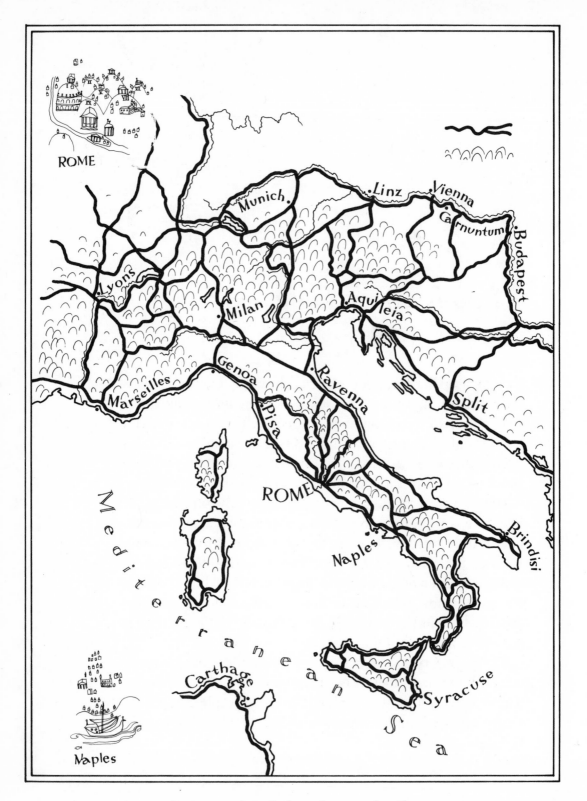

Roman roads in Italy and across the Alps

waist to keep out the fierce Scots and Picts from the north. It was, and still is, called Hadrian's Wall, though he himself allowed all to know that the work had been carried out by his legate, Aulus Platorius Nepos. It was finished in A.D. 127.

As time etched its way into his health, he completed his villa twenty-five miles from Rome. It was the most beautiful single project in all the empire. After that he began to prepare for his death.

Across the Tiber River, he had built for himself the largest and most impressive mausoleum ever built. It was solidly built and has been used as a tomb, a fortress, a castle, and a home for the popes. It still stands — Castel Sant' Angelo — as does the bridge that he built over the Tiber to lead to it.

In the rare quiet moments as death neared, the Emperor Hadrian could look back upon all that he had done to make Rome eternal. War alone had not done this. Hadrian's aim had been to consolidate what Rome had won through conquest, and bring universal peace through trade. Trade was not possible without roads, and in A.D. 138 there was a network of 53,000 miles of roads throughout the Roman world.

Eighteen of these roads entered Rome; beyond Rome these eighteen spread out like a spider's web until those who administered the roads had 324 roads, long and short, under their care. There were laws for the building of roads and laws for the repairing of roads. Men felt themselves highly honored to build a highway. The Emperor Augustus had repaved the Via Flaminia at his own expense. The people raised an arch to his honor for this public act. Hadrian paved the Via Cassia, from Rome to Florence (Florentia), at his own expense. Agrippa, the architect who had built the Pantheon in Rome and had become rich from public architecture, felt that he could best repay Rome for what she had done for him by repairing four great Alpine roads, all out of his own funds.

One of the great works of Hadrian: a 100-mile-long aqueduct in Tunisia brought water from the Zaghouan Mountains to Carthage. The underground section of the aqueduct still remains in use.

By the year of Hadrian's death, A.D. 138, the great period of road building had come to an end. For four hundred fifty years the Romans had built highways that led to the most remote areas. Unlike most capitals Rome had no need for elaborate defense walls. The wall of Servius, which had been built in the fourth century B.C., was destroyed in the sack of the capital by the Gauls in 390 B.C. Not until the third century A.D. was another wall erected around Rome to hold out the barbarians. Even today most of this wall, built by Aurelian, can be seen in Rome. After the sack of Rome, geography made it very clear that the only way to prevent tribes whom the Romans regarded as barbarians from coming down from the Alps to make raids on what Rome thought was hers was to extend Roman territory.

The first road to be built to the north was begun in 264 B.C. The Via Flaminia, this great northern road, was named after the censor Gaius Flaminius who extended it in 220 B.C. Its purpose was to move northeast to extend communications to the Adriatic Sea, 140 Roman miles from the capital. The road went to Fano (Fanum Fortunae), on the Adriatic, and then became a coastal road. Slowly the soldiers pushed north along the coast. As they conquered, the paved road followed. Twenty miles northward they reached the sea-placed city called Rimini (Ariminum).

Rimini is at the edge of the Po Valley. Italy's two largest rivers, the Po and the Adige, had created a broad, fertile

Gateway of the Via Latina as it enters the walls of Rome. The wall was begun in A.D. 271 by the Emperor Aurelian and was completed by A.D. 280.

The early Roman tunnel on the Via Flaminia at the Furlo Pass appears to the right of the larger arched tunnel also built by the Romans and still in use.

valley from which the Roman legions had to oust the Gauls, those blond-haired Alpine peoples whose "only business was fighting and farming."

Later, in the year 187 B.C., the consul M. Aemilius Lepidus was the field general. He fought against the tribes called Ligurians. As he fought, Aemilius built his road. It began at Rimini, on the Adriatic Sea, the end of the Flaminian Way, and went on as straight as the course of light to Piacenza (Placentia). When the war was finished, so was the road. It was called the Via Aemilia. One hundred eighty miles long, it carried Roman arms to the foothills of the Alps.

At the same period of history two other great roads were slowly creeping northward, and by the same method. Attack by the legions, then pacification. Then the road followed. And so did commerce.

The Via Cassia was an ancient dirt road that led to Veii, an old Etruscan city ten miles north of Rome. Then in 177 B.C., after the cities to the north had been subdued, the Romans planned to rebuild and extend the road to what is now Florence. It took thirty years of building through mountainous lands to reach Florence.

The other great artery issuing from the heart of Rome was the Via Aurelia. Three stone bridges crossed the Tiber carrying traffic from the city to the Via Aurelia, which led to the sea, twenty miles away. These were the Pons Cestius, Pons Fabricius, and Pons Aemilius. The first two were bridges in tandem, so to speak. They connected the Tiber Island with both banks of the river. The Via Aurelia was built as usual on a deep and secure foundation of crushed stone, then a

A Roman road near the town of Fiano Romano in Italy. It is one of Rome's earliest roads and went to the ancient town of Capena.

The Porta Praetoria at Aosta, built in the time of Augustus. Aosta is at the junction of the Great and the Little St. Bernard passes.

pavement of stones weighing as much as two hundred pounds each. Such a road needed little upkeep. The Aurelian Way, which now has almost totally disappeared, went as far up the coast as Luni (Luna). It kept to the seacoast. Year after year the road was extended until it went to Genoa (Genua), around the bend of the Mediterranean Sea to what is now the French coast, and into Spain.

It is not fully certain just when the Romans made their first attack on the Alps. The three northern roads, connecting with smaller ones, were built to the base of the Alps. Then, as the Romans pursued the Gauls, the roads had to go higher and higher into the snowbound Alps.

Once the Roman Senate had decided on a long-range policy to conquer all of Gaul, the legions were sent to find

*The Roman road below and the modern road above leading
to the famous St. Bernard Pass across the Alps.*

the shortest way. They went over the Alps through the highest pass, now called the Great St. Bernard Pass, 8111 feet
above sea level. The snowfall is so heavy that the road, at
least during Roman times, was closed between November
and April. But Hannibal, even though encumbered with his
elephants, had crossed the Alps. Why not the Romans?

Proconsul for the year 120 B.C., Domitius Ahenobarbus,
financed the work himself. The land was too cold for slaves;
the Gauls could be made to work on the road only if watched
by soldiers, so the Roman legions built it. It was a narrow
road, not much more than eight feet wide, made of two
layers of rammed gravel between thick keystone-shaped
stones. Still it was the first Roman road to cross the Alps.
On the pinnacle of the pass the Romans built a temple to

Jupiter Poeninus, and close to it a large hospice to give people who used the road a resting place. It also housed people whose job it was to rescue those who were lost in the snow.

In 60 B.C. Rome came under the power of three men; called a "triumvirate," the rule of three, the three were Pompey, Crassus, and Julius Caesar.

Crassus was an ambitious millionaire. "No one can be considered rich," he said, "who cannot afford to pay for his own army." Crassus also spent a great deal for the repairing of roads and bridges out of his own purse.

Julius Caesar had begun his official career in Rome as the overseer of the Via Appia. This brought him to the attention of the Senate. He became known as an excellent administrator. To make the rule of the three closer, Caesar gave his daughter in marriage to Pompey, the last of "the three."

Pompey was a brilliant soldier, the best since Scipio. He had fought in Hither Asia, Spain, and against the Gauls. He had moved his legions and his engineers to the Alps to find a shorter route to Gaul. The Great St. Bernard Pass was closed during the winter months, so Pompey had ordered his pioneers to search for the roads used by the Gauls, and the one that Hannibal must have taken when he crossed the Alps in 218 B.C. to attack Italy.

Pompey built the second Roman road across the Alps. It began in Turin (Taurasia) in Italy, crossed the col now known as the San Bernardino, the Little St. Bernard, and then down the other side into Gaul, where it came to a halt at a well-placed area that they called Vienna, present-day Vienne.

As Julius Caesar's share of the "rule of three" he asked, and received, the command of Gaul. The whole land vaguely known as Gaul is more or less within the boundaries of present-day France. In 57 B.C. Julius Caesar marched his

Roman roads in Gaul

legions over Pompey's road into Gaul. As it was not wide enough for all of this transport, he had his legate, Fabius Valens, rebuild it.

Within three years, as Julius Caesar himself has related, he conquered all of Gaul. This action brought him up to the Rhine River, the natural boundary between Gaul and Germany. He built the first bridge across the Rhine, near present-day Coblenz (Confluentes). His own description of it is so complete that historians were able to reconstruct a model of the bridge. It was a quarter of a mile long. First he sank two rows of piles, joined in pairs, in the river. The rows sloped inward, "so made," wrote Caesar of his design, "that the greater thrust of the water, the tighter the balks held." On these slanted piles his engineers laid wooden beams. Then over these a wickerwork of light wood and on top of this the road itself, made of mixed mud and gravel that would be hardened by the heat of the sun.

In time—for just as Rome was not built in one day, neither were its roads—in time the whole of Gaul was crisscrossed with finely laid roads. So well laid were these roads that once Julius Caesar, when called to do so, was able to travel in a chariot one hundred miles in a day.

The road from Turin, in Italy, going over the Alps to Briançon (Brigantio), and from there on to Vienne, Lyons (Lugdunum), Paris (Lutetia), and the channel port of Boulogne-sur-Mer (Gesoriacum), was the great highway to Britain.

In 46 B.C. the Romans founded the city of Arles (Arelas) in Southern France, and in time they built there massive theaters, temples, and colosseums that still stand intact today. In 19 B.C., Agrippa built the famous aqueduct and bridge called the Pont du Gard in Provence, and although it no longer conveys water it still stands as an eternal monument to the Romans' engineering genius.

Augustus, heir of Julius Caesar

Octavian followed Julius Caesar. He was nineteen years old at the time of his great-uncle's death. "Octavian was born," said a Roman historian, "before sunrise on the ninth day before the kalends of October . . . at the sign of the Oxheads in Rome." He was educated to simple tastes, liked neither pomp nor ceremony. He knew, however, how to obtain power and how to hold it. In the civil war that followed Caesar's death, most of the public works, including the building of roads, came to a halt.

Mark Antony became a successful general in the lands around the Mediterranean, and although he was married to Octavian's sister, he put her aside and took instead the famous Cleopatra. This in itself did not bring on civil war, but soon the two consuls made war upon each other. It ended in the suicides of Cleopatra and Antony.

In 27 B.C. Octavian assumed the name of Augustus and became in his terms "princeps," but in other people's thought "the emperor." With the peace that his firm hand brought to

Rome, a Rome wearied by so much war and death, building began at a fevered pace. Rome had grown so immense that it needed reorganization. For each function Augustus chose a director. There was a director of roads, one for aqueducts, since there were seven large aqueducts bringing water into Rome, another for public works.

Until Augustus' time, no one had devoted himself so much to the care and extension of Roman roads. This expanded program was one of the reasons for Rome's new prosperity, which flowed into all ranks of life. There had been a time when Cicero had called the 300,000 common people of Rome "the dregs of Romulus." Until then it had been true. Now peace and prosperity came to the lands. There were new woolen mills in Pompeii, fine pottery came out of Campania, metal-working guilds appeared in Rome and in Milan (Mediolanum) to the north. The port of Ostia, at the mouth of the Tiber, was filled with ships carrying exports from Rome. In turn ships came in from all over the Roman world, bringing in new luxuries. The river traffic was so crowded that Augustus had to improve the roads to the port.

The Via Portuensis, called so because it led to the port, was built to take care of the direct traffic to the sea. The other road, called the Via Ostiensis, led to the city of Ostia.

Ostia began to build up rapidly as men grew rich from trade. It seemed at one time to rival Rome. There were numerous four-storied apartments, called *insulae*, bound on all four sides by sidewalks. Shops faced well-paved stone-laid streets, there were public toilets, theaters, baths, and in Ostia alone four public libraries. Back of the amphitheater was one of the forums. Around it under the shaded colonnades were the offices of the various trading centers of the empire. In front of each office, in black and white mosaic, were the symbols and names of each trading center. Libya was sym-

The elephant of Libya, a mosaic from Ostia where the agents for each of the Roman provinces had their offices.

bolized by an elephant, Marseilles by a bridge, the island of Sicily by a wild boar.

Ostia grew rich on the imported wheat for the million people of Rome. It was their staple. Romans lived on porridge. It was monotonous, and for the poor it was relieved only by vegetables—olives, herbs, mushrooms, onions, and especially garlic; rarely could they afford pork, salted and spiced with rosemary leaves. Elephant flesh could be purchased, but meat from cattle was eaten only when an ox was sacrificed.

Life was far different for the wealthy Romans. They prepared fashionable dinners with six or seven courses; hors d'oeuvres of small birds, mushrooms, radishes, eggs, oysters, and sardines. Most people drank wine thinned with water. A heavier drink, a form of mead, came from fermented honey.

Coffee, although it was discovered in Ethiopia, was never drunk. Tea seems to have been known to the Romans, since they traded with India, but no one ever mentions using it. All this might seem lean fare at the present time, yet there were so many different Roman dishes that cookbooks were available. *The Art of Cookery* has survived until today. A translation of this cookbook appeared in English in 1958. The two women who did the work not only translated but tried out many of the recipes. (*The Art of Cookery*, by Barbara Flower, London, 1958.)

VII

A Roman road in Vienne, France

Highways of Empire

One of the other reasons why Rome prospered under Augustus was the care with which money was minted. Augustus made certain that his master of the mint was honest. Each piece of money, whether it be copper, silver, or gold, contained the standard amount of metal. As most of the coinage of Augustus was silver, Rome turned to the province of Spain, a plenteous source, for it.

The first Roman colony in Spain was founded at Italica in 205 B.C. Great battles had been fought in Spain between the Romans and the Celts, on the one hand, and the Romans against the Carthaginians, on the other. Each used the conquered peoples as troops. It was from Spain that Hannibal set off with his army and war elephants to conquer Rome. And it was in Spain that Marcus Cato first made his reputation. In 195 B.C. he commanded several legions there.

There were extensive silver mines in Cartagena (Carthago Nova), on the coast of Spain. So great were the silver deposits that one Roman remembers seeing forty thousand slaves working one of the silver mines.

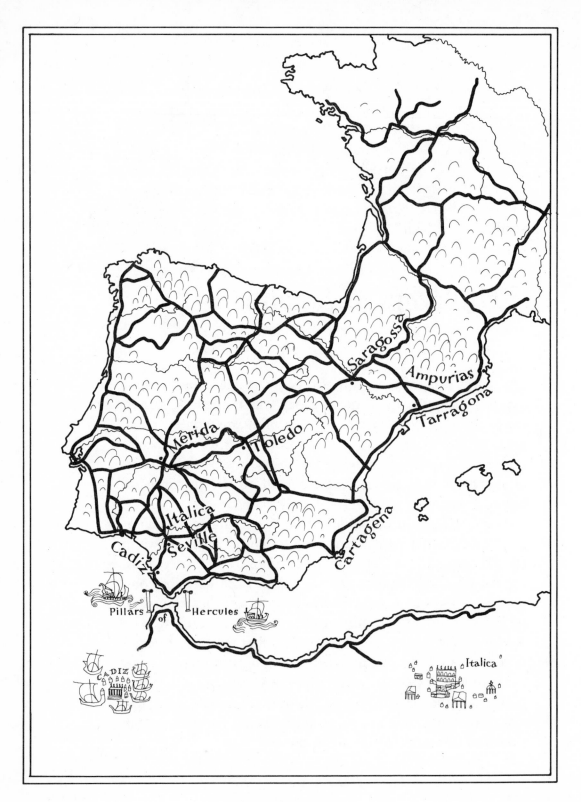

Roman roads in Spain

The road that led to Spain was in reality a continuation of the Via Aurelia, which led out of Rome. Under different names, it went north along the coast of Italy and rounded the southern coast of France into the ancient port of Massilia, now called Marseilles. From Marseilles the road went down the Spanish coast, passing that part of the coast where the rock-bound Pyrenees come down to the sea. Once the road entered Spain, it took the name of Via Augusta. By 8 B.C. it had reached the town of Saragossa (Caesaraugusta).

Julius Caesar had Romanized Southern Spain. Augustus opened the communications to the interior.

What became the Via Augusta had been started in 120 B.C. and was then called the Via Herculia. The work in Spain, as in Italy, was slow and costly because the land was mountainous. Stone retaining walls had to be constructed before roads were laid down; every stream had to be bridged.

By the year 1 B.C. it could be confirmed to the emperor that the road bearing his name had entered Cartagena. The governor of the city announced that he would now be able to send back to Rome, for its silver coinage, more metal than had ever been sent in the previous centuries, which even then had been as much as 130,000 pounds of silver a year.

Gades, the modern city of Cádiz, lies west of Gibraltar, and beyond the Pillars of Hercules. It had been famed as an ancient trading center and was the last port of call for ships before they ventured out into the uncharted Atlantic. The new Roman road, the Via Argenta, or silver road, went from Gades inland to Italica. It was here that the Emperors Trajan and Hadrian were born. Many other famed Romans were born in Spain; best remembered are the dramatist and essayist Seneca, who had the misfortune to be the tutor of Nero, and Balbus, who was sent to Africa to defend Rome against the onrushing desert hordes. From Italica the Via Argenta went on to the larger Roman colony of Augusta Emerita, present-day Mérida.

There were seven principal roads in Spain, built between 160 B.C. and A.D. 383, and numerous smaller ones, thirty-four in all, added to the Roman road system.

The records, taken mostly from the milestones, show that thirty-five emperors between 32 B.C. and A.D. 383 built, rebuilt, or repaired the Roman roads in Spain.

Some of these were tyrants of the worst sort. Caracalla, the curly-bearded emperor who reigned for only six short years, was famed for his tiresome and dangerous personality, and yet the records show that in A.D. 214 he ordered the rebuilding of many of the major roads in Spain. It is amazing that the pride of building roads was in even him. He personally led his armies to the Danube, then began a campaign in Scotland beyond the confines of Hadrian's Wall. He made a brief visit to Spain in A.D. 214, long enough to issue the decree for the rebuilding of all the roads. In A.D. 212 he made world citizens of all who were living within the boundaries of the Roman Empire:

"Edict of the Emperor Caesar Marcus Aurelius Antoninus Augustus [Caracalla]. To divine power I refer the reasons and considerations whereby I should worthily show my gratitude to the gods for preserving me in safety in the midst of great peril. I believe I can render proper service to their majesty in dignified and reverent worship if I bring as many myriads as owe me obedience to share in sacrifice to the gods. Accordingly I bestow Roman citizenship on all my subjects throughout the world, no one except *dediticii* [freedmen, slaves set free] being denied citizens' rights. It is proper that my people should share not only the common burdens but also the joy of my victory. This ordinance shall extend the might of the Roman people since the distinction for which Romans have been honored has now been granted to others."

Caracalla, son of Septimius Severus

During the long reign of Augustus there was a peace, but a troubled one. Along the Rhine, for one place. While the legions did not attempt to make further conquests beyond the Rhine, it was their custom to make a military parade of strength. One day in April, A.D. 9, the commanding general, Varus, was asked to make a punitive expedition into those great silent forests which clothed that part of the world. The legions were to punish the murderers of a tax collector. It was a trap, planned by Hermann, whose name had been Romanized into Arminius, an officer on the staff of Varus. His loyalty had been unquestioned. He had been to Rome and had been enrolled among the Roman knights. As was Rome's policy, any of the conquered who wished to be Romanized could do so and receive all the honors and duties of Roman citizens.

Once the legions were locked in the gloomy forests, the dirt roads turned into a morass and their wagon trains

bogged down in the mud. Then the Alemanni attacked. Of
the three legions, numbering more than twelve thousand
men, only one officer, named Cassius Chaerea, with a few
men, was able to fight his way out. Had he not, no one would
have been aware of the fate of the legions of Varus. The
Roman standards, on which were engraved the eagle, the
symbol of Rome, and the victories and the names of the
legions, were captured. Symbols and men disappeared into
the gloom of death.

In Rome there was panic. Augustus was then seventy years
of age; he was unprepared for so great a loss in Roman arms
and Roman prestige. It is said that he would wake in the
night and call out:

"Varus, where are my legions, bring me back my legions."

It is also said he had a map of the Empire engraved on a
sheet of gold and studded with small jewels to mark the cities.
It hung in his room. After the ambush of his legions he called
Drusus, his stepson, in charge of all the Roman troops in
Gaul and beyond. He was told to find another pass and build
a new secret highway across the Alps so that the newly formed
legions could attack the Alemanni.

The Via Drusia was begun at the base of the Dolomite
Alps at Bolzano (Bauzanum). The whole area is mountainous
and the Romans had to employ every available person. The
pioneers followed the Adige River. It flows past Bolzano
through a wide valley. Beyond, to the north, is Merano,
where the Adige turns abruptly westward, and upward.

On all sides the Alps tower over the plunging Adige, and
countless rills, pouring down from them, help to swell the
river in its path downward. When the valley began to narrow
the engineers had to pry the stone out of the mountain
in order to make a base for the road. The Adige, they found,
had its origin in two small lakes, ice-fringed most of the year.

Tiberius, heir of Augustus

At 4900 feet they found the pass the Celts called "Reschen Pass." Today it is known as the Reschen Scheideck Pass. Parts of a Roman tunnel can still be seen even though it was two thousand years ago that the legions of Drusus pierced the rock. On one side of the Alps the Adige River flows south into the Adriatic Sea. On the other side the Inn River flows through the heartland of Austria and empties into the Danube.

The Via Drusia gave the legions another way over the Alps to attack the barbarians who constantly kept the soldiers and the frontiers in turmoil.

Then came the turn of Tiberius, the brother of Drusus. He was a battle-scarred veteran. He was born in 42 B.C. and had seen action as a soldier at sixteen. He had been a military tribune in Spain. At twenty-two he commanded in Armenia, and at twenty-nine he was made a consul at Rome. So pleased was the Emperor Augustus with him that he gave him his daughter Julia as his wife. But this did not make Tiberius very happy, and when he was sent to distant lands, he was at least pleased to escape his wife as well as his imperious mother.

Tiberius was a soldier's soldier. He shared the dangers and discomforts of his own men. He was efficient. When war came he kept at it doggedly until victory was certain. Soldiers were never allowed to be idle; Tiberius knew that sloth brought on a lack of discipline. It was his plan to make them builders of roads.

The soldiers grumbled and once revolted, but they did build roads throughout all the seasons. They quarried the rock, carried it to the roads, cut it, and put it in place. They cut trees, built retaining walls, bridges, causeways, viaducts, and set up milestones after having paced out each road mile for mile.

Tiberius was sent with his legions to "pacify" those lands which lay east of the Julian Alps. He was to crush the tribes of Noricum and Pannonia, lands that today are part of Austria, Hungary, and Yugoslavia. Tiberius chose as his base the seaport of Aquileia. This once great trading center has only recently been uncovered. The modern city of the same name now stands upon it, at the very northern end of the Adriatic Sea. As a port, it was well protected from the unseasonable winds that blew up the Adriatic from the south. Big ships could enter the large lagoon of Marano and find good anchorage.

Aquileia had been founded in 181 B.C. as a Roman trading colony. The name of the colony meant "eagle." Tradition had it that while the town was being laid out by a plow, which was the custom, an eagle kept hovering overhead. Four important roads led into Aquileia. One, the Via Postumia, came from the Po Valley by way of Verona and Treviso (Tarvisium).

To the north, the road that Tiberius was building, the Via
Julia Augusta, was being pushed across to a mountain village
called Sancticum, where there were hot springs. It is now
called Villach, in Austria. Near Villach in the still-virgin
woodlands can be seen clearly the narrow but well-preserved
Via Tiberia, as it came to be known, a paved road that has
withstood two thousand winters. This was the road built for
the pacification, or conquest, of Noricum.

A third road led easterly from Aquileia toward the Sava
River in what is now Yugoslavia. On its banks Augustus
ordered that a colony be built, which he called Emona.
Legend says that it had first been settled by Jason while
searching for the Golden Fleece. From Emona the road
went toward Rumania, known to the Romans as Dacia.

The fourth and most important road leaving Aquileia was

Part of the Via Julia Augusta in Aquileia on the Adriatic Sea

Roman fragments from the once great city of Salona, near Split in Yugoslavia, consist of a trefoil design for a water drain, part of a roof ornament, and broken columns.

the Via Egnatia. It was built, or at least begun, after the founding of Aquileia in 181 B.C. It is one of the longest Roman roads, going from that city all the way through mountainous Yugoslavia, bridging eighty-seven rivers, large and small. It proceeded into what today is Albania, and Greece. On the banks of the river Meric the Emperor Hadrian later built a beautiful city that he called Hadrianapolis, later called Adrianople. Then the road went down to the strait of the Bosporus into Turkey, where the second Roman capital, Constantinople, modern Istanbul, was established in A.D. 330.

Very little is mentioned in history about the Egnatian Way. Yet when Rome became split into two empires in the fourth century this road was the vital link between the emperors of the east and the west. Armies marched and countermarched over this road in support of each other.

As before, as soon as the Roman legions conquered a region, they set up first a fortress, then taverns; the Roman road followed. Within two years Tiberius had brought his legions up to the Danube. They built a fortress at what is now the city of Vienna. By A.D. 15 all Noricum was added to the empire. Trade was opened up with Carnuntum, on the Danube, where there are still remains of Roman buildings and a large amphitheater. All these areas soon were linked by road to Aquileia on the shores of the Adriatic Sea. At the end of the Noricum conquest in A.D. 14, Augustus died and Tiberius was made Roman emperor.

One hundred years later the Romans were still building roads and repairing old ones in Noricum.

In A.D. 101 the Emperor Trajan personally led his armies to the banks of the Danube to subdue the Dacians. He had with him one of the mightiest armies that ever marched along the Roman roads. The Danube had to be crossed, and Trajan began with a pontoon bridge such as Julius Caesar had put across the Rhine. But the Danube was too wide and the bridge could easily be destroyed. So Trajan sent for Apollodorus.

The amphitheater at Pulj (Pietas Julia) in Yugoslavia

TRAJAN · APOLLODORUS

Apollodorus was a Syrian from Damascus. When Trajan was governor of that province, he had met the Syrian. Everywhere Trajan went Apollodorus, his architect, followed. When cities had to be planned or bridges built, Apollodorus put his assistants to work. Trajan, born in Spain, and Apollodorus, born in Damascus, stood on the muddy shores of the Danube River and pondered if it could be bridged. The river was deep and swift, with a muddy bottom.

It was the greatest engineering project and the most daring the Romans had ever attempted. Trajan, who had pushed Rome's frontiers farther than anyone before him, thought it the greatest single thing he had ever accomplished. A replica of the bridge was later carved on Trajan's Column, designed by the same Apollodorus who built the bridge. It can still be seen occupying a prominent place on the column, which was raised to honor Trajan's conquest of the Dacians. The bridge was built on stone piers. They were sixty feet high and one hundred seventy feet apart. The whole bridge was a little over a mile in length and, except for the piers, was made of wood. It stood high above the raging Danube.

In Gaul, now peacefully under Roman rule, great cities such as Orange (Arausio), Arles, and Nîmes (Nemausus) were springing up in the south, the area called Provence (Provincia). It became a favorite of the Romans and they built many villas there. In the principal city of Gaul, Lugdunum, known today as Lyons, two of the future emperors were born. In 10 B.C., the 743rd year after the foundation of Rome, Tiberius Claudius Drusus Nero Germanicus was born in Lyons. One of the Claudii, a famous family who had given soldiers and consuls to Rome for centuries, this particular Claudius seemed the least likely to become ruler.

In Vaison la Romaine in Provence, a single arched bridge
still in use to all traffic crosses the River Ouveze

He was known as "Claudius the Stammerer." He could not get out his first name without tying up his tongue. He was always, it seemed, in ill health. He sickened easily at the sight of blood and usually fainted at the colosseum when animals were locked in mortal combat with men. In an age when every man was a soldier, he was unable even to mount a horse. Had Claudius been born among the simple people, he would have been put to death at birth. This form of euthanasia needed only the verbal testimony of six people who thought that the newly born child was unfit to live. Claudius, however, lived to become an emperor. What he did not have in physical prowess he made up for in the quality of his mind. He wrote many books and was one of the most literary of all Roman rulers.

After Caligula's death Claudius was declared emperor. He became leader of the Romans in A.D. 41. A year later he ordered that the port of Ostia be rebuilt. Later Trajan had his architects rebuild the port in a hexagonal shape (it still can be seen from the air and is now a lake set in the middle of a villa). It was to have lighthouses, temples, emporiums, barracks, custom offices, warehouses, storage bins. It was considered one of the greatest engineering works of its kind.

Claudius also rebuilt the Via Ostiensis, which led to the port. No sooner had the project been started than Claudius turned his attention north, to the Alps. Why no one had thought of using the Brenner Pass as a means of passing over the Alps is not known. Claudius looked at the huge map, etched in stone, that Augustus had made of the roads leading to all the places in the empire. He noticed one thing. The shortest distance to Noricum was at the place where the land height was the lowest. It was called the Brenner Pass, named after Brennus, a Gallic chieftain. The pass, which was only 4494 feet above sea level, was constantly open. The legions

The Emperor Claudius.
He adopted Nero as his heir,
setting aside his own son
Britannicus

followed the river that the Gauls called the Eisack, and there in easy passage reached the pass.

To go down the other side to the Inn River was a matter of rapid descent of only fifty miles. At the Inn the Romans built a bridge, famous for centuries. The fortress village became in time Innsbruck, the place where the bridge crossed the Inn River. This became a favorite way for the Roman legions, and the drayers who brought their wagons and carts over the high road.

By A.D. 43 it had been almost a century since Julius Caesar had made his swift conquest of Britain. However only a corner, the southeastern part, was under Roman control. Claudius perhaps believed that an invasion of Britain would bring his name a renown that it did not yet have. He knew from military intelligence that many of the Britons around York (Eboracum) were very heavily armed and that they had well-made war chariots and heavy armor. He decided to bring war elephants on his conquest.

Elephants were becoming a common sight in Rome. They were brought over from Africa and used for heavy work. And elephant meat was offered for sale. When Nero moved the colossal monument of himself to the Flavian Amphitheater, twenty-four elephants were used to pull the immense monument into place. There had been a fight at the games between a rhinoceros and an elephant. People thought that the rhino, because of his thick hide and long, sharp horn, would make short work of the elephant. The elephant tried to penetrate the hide of the rhino to no avail. Then, spying a broom left by one of the workmen, he took it in his trunk and when the rhino charged he stuck the sharp bristles into his eyes, blinding him. In rage, anger, and pain the rhino ran into the wooden barrier and knocked himself senseless.

Claudius, whose frail body made him depend more on his sharp wits than on his body, appreciated the native intelligence of the elephant. But Roman generals were not overly impressed with war elephants. After all, Hannibal arrived with only one single elephant after crossing the Alps. He had started across with thirty-seven. Protected by armor and using bells, the Romans learned how to stampede the elephants. It was dangerous since the elephants could end up by trampling to death more friends than foes.

The troops selected for the invasion of Britain were chosen from the Legio II Augusta, which had served on the Rhine and was used to the type of warfare that would be encountered in Britain; the Spanish contingent, the IX Hispania, which had just served in Pannonia on the Danube; and two other legions, stationed in Lower Germany. The legions landed unopposed on the shore of Britain. Then the swift chariots of the Britons came down upon them. But discipline won the day, and the charioteers were defeated. The slaughter was awesome.

The battles, without quarter, went on for some years. Claudius, usually ill with ague and chilblains, did not stay in the field all of those years. He took command of the army beyond the Thames and in sixteen action-packed days forced countless unnamed tribes into surrender. The rest was a soldier's battle—grim, hard hand-to-hand fighting, ambush and burnings. Eventually Britain was won. Then, as elsewhere, lands won by the sword were consolidated by roads, which brought trade and peace.

The Roman roads in England were carefully planned, even though the Romans then had neither map nor compass. In order to sight a road they used the *groma*. An alignment was laid out and workers went ahead to fell the trees. As the land of Britain was then, as it is now, moist and rainy, the engineers built up embankments, in a word, a highway. The name for the ditch, or embankment, was *agger*. On this they built or laid down the road. The thickness of the stone depended on the type of road; usually two or three feet of crushed stone rammed down was enough. The surface of the road was high in the center so that rain, which fell incessantly, would run off into the ditch.

Some but not all roads were metaled, that is, paved with stone slabs as most of the roads were in Italy. The important roads were twenty-four feet wide, the lesser ones kept to a width of fifteen feet, wide enough for two wagons to pass without striking one another. Eight main roads went out from London (Londinium) like the spokes of a wheel. All had names, without doubt, but most of these roads have disappeared. There are still a Port Way, a Fosse Way, and streets

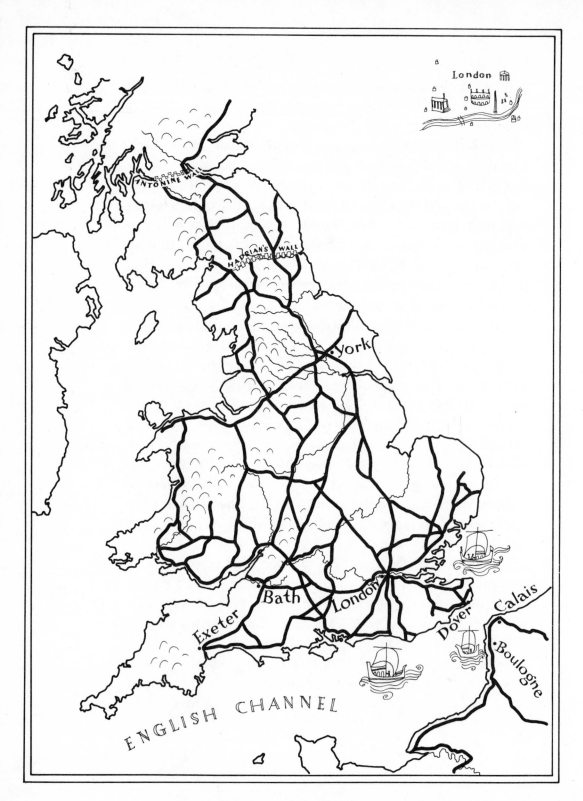

Roman roads in Britain

such as Watling Street, which was the principal way from Dover, where the Romans maintained a tall lighthouse, seventy miles or more from London.

London was the hub and center of the road system. Roads went out and all over Britain. No one knows who built the first bridge across the Thames. Doubtless it was a pontoon bridge such as Julius Caesar erected across the Rhine. Somehow the elephants had to get over, but no one speaks much about the war elephants. After the first shock the Britons must have allowed time and the British climate to take care of the warmth-loving elephants.

A road went to Wales to get to the deposits of copper and coal, and north to York to open the lead mines and obtain sheep's wool and mutton.

As usual the Romans were preoccupied with health. They had a positive nose for water and spas. They found one at Aquae Solis, known for centuries simply as Bath. Here waters issued from the earth at 120°. Over and around the springs they built an impressive building. Architects were brought from Rome to construct it, and much of it still remains.

Each community took care of the part of the Roman road that entered its boundaries. Each canton was required to provide material and labor gangs. The conquered Britons naturally complained that their conquerors forced them to work on the highways. Road-working started many a local revolt. Galgacus, chief of a clan of Caledonians, in Northern Britain, exhorted his people to revolt. He complained to the Roman general Julius Agricola that "the Romans consume our hands and bodies in making roads through woods and marshes, striking us if we do not work, and cursing us while they are doing it."

The Romans did not relent. What joy was it to walk or

Hadrian's Wall, built in northern Britain to hold back Picts and Scots

ride over bogs and marshes when one could travel over a well-kept road? Before the Romans came to the island, to journey there was like a fragment of hell. Whereas a Roman road made it possible for the traveler to move over the surface of the land as a civilized being.

The roads were served by an imperial post system. At least sixteen of the principal routes had such services. Coaches, four-wheeled wagons, and two-wheeled courier gigs traveled back and forth. About every twelve or fifteen miles there were *mutationes*, where horses were changed. At the same distance, or perhaps a little farther, between eighteen and twenty miles, there were resthouses called *mansiones*. Next to the *mansiones* some enterprising person, a merchant or a retired

Hadrian, heir of Trajan,
emperor A.D. *117-138*

soldier who had been given an allotment of land, would put up a *taberna*, or tavern, where the traveler could eat, drink, and sleep.

Between 50 B.C. and A.D. 350 Rome built and improved the road system, until in time Britain had a network of over six thousand miles of all-weather roads.

In A.D. 122 the Emperor Hadrian came to Britain. He had been traveling all over the Roman realm for thirteen years, putting bounds to his empire. He gave up land in Asia, putting up pillars to mark the Roman domain at the Euphrates. He dismantled the famous bridge across the Danube. He had been in Lower Germany where he built an immense line of fortifications.

Hadrian arrived to put bounds to Roman ambitions in Britain. A Roman legion had been wiped out in Northern Britain. Unless the fierce highlanders could be contained, the lowlands would be overrun. For more than one hundred years the Romans had tried without success to subdue the Picts and the Scots. Hadrian built a wall to keep them back.

His engineers anchored the wall at Wallsend on the Tyne. Built of rubble and cement, it was fifteen feet high and seventy-six miles long, ending at Bowness on the Solway Firth. Every Roman mile was marked with a milecastle, complete with barracks, forum, baths, and officers' quarters. In front of the wall was a deep inclining ditch. Attackers would have to expose themselves in going up the slant and again when they went down into the ditch. If they attacked a portion of the wall, Roman foot soldiers and horsemen sallied out from the milecastles to attack them.

In the year of his death, A.D. 138, Hadrian had his secretaries review all that had been done. He believed, but time proved him wrong, that Rome could hold her empire by setting bounds to it. He is reported to have said:

"Catastrophe and ruin will fall one day on Rome . . . but order will come too . . . not all of our books shall perish and some few men will think and work and feel as we have done . . ."

VIII

The bridge of Alcántara in Spain

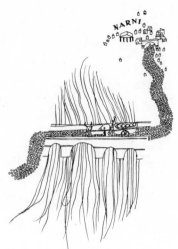

The Bridge,
Little Brother of the Road

The Romans were not the inventors of the bridge. No one knows where the first bridge appeared or when; still, the Romans were the perfecters of it. In order to maintain over 53,000 miles of all-weather roads, the Romans had to build and maintain over two thousand bridges, bridges as small as the twenty-foot arch that crossed the famous Rubicon, and as large as the mile-long Danube bridge. At no point in history, until now, in the last decades of this century, have any people anywhere dealt with nature on so grand a scale.

No matter how perfect a road or how well maintained, if the smallest bridge on a road becomes impassable, the entire road ceases to function.

Rivers change their course with callous ease. The builder of a bridge must know where the thrust of the water may come. If not, the finest bridge, if it is not properly protected from the power of water, will come tumbling down. The

137

Pontoon bridge depicted on column of Marcus Aurelius.

Egyptians had no bridges, save logs thrown across irrigation streams. No one has ever seen the remains of a Greek bridge, although the Greek poet Homer seems to talk as if bridges were common in his time.

The first stone bridge on record is the one that the architect of Babylon, named Nabopolassar, built across the Euphrates River in the sixth century B.C. The bridge was 380 feet long and rested on seven streamlined piers of baked brick. The actual bridge was built of wood.

Darius the Great, at war with the Scythians about 512 B.C., built a bridge across the Bosporus. Even the name of the builder of the bridge is remembered. "I, Mandrokles of Samia, built this bridge . . ." It was destroyed.

Then in 481 B.C. Xerxes, the son of Darius, built a pontoon bridge across the two-mile-wide strait that joins the Aegean Sea with the Sea of Marmara. At these narrows, which separate Asia Minor from Europe, is the Hellespont.

Near the town of Abydos in Asia Minor, Xerxes's bridge was to cross the water to the Greek town of Sestos. A fleet of shallow boats, the pontoons, was brought up, and the boats were laced together by cables, one made from flax, the other from papyrus. But the bridge was scarcely laid down when a storm came, broke the cables, and smashed the boats. Xerxes was furious. He ordered that the Hellespont be given three hundred lashes. As the storm whirled about him, he cursed:

"You salted and bitter stream. Your master Xerxes lays this punishment upon you . . . But Xerxes the King will cross you, with or without permission." And he ordered the bridge to be rebuilt.

"The method," said Herodotus, the Greek historian born about 484 B.C., "was to lash 360 galleys together. They were moored with heavy anchors and large gaps were allowed between them to assure passage of ships from the Aegean to the Black Sea. The cables attached to the ships were hauled taut by wooden winches on the sides of both shores. Next, wooden planks cut in lengths equal to the width of the floating ships were laid down and secured. On top of this, light brushwood was laid down and then a layer of clay which was trodded down and smoothed. Finally a paling or railing was put up on both sides to prevent mules or horses from falling into the water."

The Romans built their first bridge before they built their first stone-laid road. This was the famous Pons Sublicius, a pile bridge made entirely of wood, hence its name from Latin *sublices*, wooden beams. It was built, according to the legend, in the seventh century B.C. by Ancus Marcius, one of the Latin kings of Rome. Since the bridges were always sacred, the structure was put into the hands of the high priest of Rome; his title was *pontifex*, bridgemaker. Eventually the word was changed to pontiff, a title inherited by the popes, who "bridge" life and death. It was this Pons Sublicius that Horatius defended "at the bridge." Who will forget the poet

writing how, as the Etruscan army neared the north bank of
the Tiber, Horatius held them off while Rome's first bridge
was destroyed:

> Then out spake brave Horatius,
> The Captain of the Gate:
> "To every man upon this earth
> Death cometh soon or late" . . .

*Ruins of the first stone bridge in Rome, the Pons Aemilius,
known today as the Ponte Rotto, the broken bridge. Existing
arches are mainly medieval. In background, is Pons Fabricius.*

Detail of the Pons Fabricius with the name and title of the builder cut into the stone: L. Fabricius, curator viarum.

While the Romans attacked the foundation of the bridge to bring it down, Horatius and two companions held off the attacking Etruscans. None could pass the ten-foot-wide bridge.

Another Pons Sublicius took its place in time. Three additional bridges were erected in the first century. The first stone bridge was finished in 142 B.C., just a few years after the destruction of Carthage.

The famed bridge of Fabricius, which crossed from the city to the Tiber Island, was constructed about 62 B.C. by

L. Fabricius, after whom it was named. It has two semi-circular arches and was made from volcanic rock and covered with limestone.

The Pons Aemilius, also called the Senatorum, was built below the Tiber Island to carry traffic directly across the river to the Via Aurelia. In all, eight bridges were built between 142 B.C. and A.D. 300 across the Tiber. The most famed, and still carrying thousands of tons of traffic daily, is the Milvian Bridge. It is the largest, with eight arches. It was built in 109 B.C. to connect with the Via Flaminia and all of the other north-bound roads that lead off at the bridge.

In constructing their bridges, the Roman engineers used the same methods used today. To sink the foundation of a pier, they made a cofferdam around the site of the pier. They drove in piles to make the dam, then pumped out the water. They dug out the silt until they reached rock bottom. Then they dug out the rock and cemented their huge ashlars to the base rock.

As early as 300 B.C. the Romans had discovered cement. Around Vesuvius there were vast deposits of sandy volcanic ash. They called it *pulvis Puteolanus* because it was first found in the seaport called Puteoli, close to present-day Naples. The Roman engineers found that this volcanic ash, when added to lime mortar, sand, or gravel and water, made a cement as hard as stone. It even hardened under water. This was one of the keys to their success in bridgebuilding. The other was the perfection of the arch. The Greeks knew of it, but they seldom made use of it. The Etruscans gave it to the Romans. The Romans learned the use of the arch and the dome. With the arch and cement, Roman bridges could span large spaces. Once the principal rules were understood, there was little they would not take on.

On the Roman highways, bridges, viaducts, and causeways

became common. In A.D. 98 Trajan built the twenty-mile-long causeway over the Pontine Marshes. His engineers assembled a large fleet of old boats, filled them with rocks, then sank them in line. With these as a base, large piles were driven into the marsh bottom and between these rock was inserted. The causeway rose six feet above the flood level of the marshes.

The farther from Rome the roads led, the greater were the bridge problems. On the Via Flaminia, at the river Nera at the town of Narni, Augustus built one of the most impressive bridges in Italy. It was built in 16 B.C. and had six arches. The main arch had a span of 139 feet.

Agrippa, the great builder of Augustus, built the famed Pont du Gard. This is a great aqueduct-bridge that crosses

The Pont du Gard, built by Agrippa in 19 B.C. in Provence. It no longer carries water but has been converted into a bridge.

Roman bridge in Narbonne, France, early colony of Narbo Martius.

the valley of the Gard, in Southern France. It is composed of an arcade of six arches, stands 160 feet high, and is about 900 feet in length. It not only had utility, but it had beauty. It still stands in its entirety.

No one has ever sat down to figure out exactly the number of Roman bridges still in use, but someone has arrived at an approximate figure of 185. Who can say? Who has traveled over all the 53,000 miles of Roman roads and put down the remains he has seen? No one. There are two thousand or more rivers and rills that were crossed by Roman roads in Italy alone; all had to be bridged.

Tunisia, in North Africa, half desert and yet famed for

being the wheat belt of Rome, has thirty bridges, some as immense as those erected in Italy. In France and in some parts of Yugoslavia, Roman bridges are still used.

Spain, of all the countries that were part of the Roman Empire, has the greatest number of original Roman bridges still in use.

In 24 B.C., the Emperor Augustus returned from Spain. In 25 B.C. he had ordered that the doors of the Temple of Janus in Rome be closed. This signified a time of peace. Not quite so, yet enough to mark the beginning of the Pax Romana.

Augustus built or had built during his long reign many of the principal roads. Of the 372 Roman roads listed in the world at the end of the fourth century A.D., more than 34 were in Spain. Spain is like Italy, mountainous. And the roads were difficult to build and to maintain. The principal road that ran along the coast, now called the Costa Brava, from France into Spain was rebuilt by Augustus. Eight large bridges had to be built along this route.

The Via Argenta, the silver road (the Spaniards later translated it as "Camino de la Plata," meaning the same thing), led to Italica, then to Mérida. This city was founded by Augustus in 23 B.C. and was planned as the capital of an entire Spanish province; eight roads converged on the city to form a hub of communications. Leading into Mérida, one of the greatest bridges in Spain was built by the Roman engineers. It crosses the Guadiana River. It has sixty arches, is over a half mile in length, and was so well constructed that it is still in use. Four bridges built in Spain in the time of Augustus are still in use.

Northward from Mérida the silver road goes to Salamanca (Salamantica). It is a city famed throughout history for its beauty. Its university is one of the oldest. Hernando Cortez, the conqueror of Aztec Mexico, studied law there for some months. Salamanca was also famed as a Roman colony and for its bridge. The bridge has twenty-seven arches and has been able to stand for all these two thousand years, even though the Tormes River, which it crosses, brings down torrents of water.

Yet the most celebrated bridge in Spain is the Alcántara. The word is Arabic and means the bridge. It is obvious why it is called "The Bridge." It is on the road from Mérida and leads to Portugal, which in the time of the Romans was known as Lusitania. The Tagus River, which it crossed, was an unruly stream with deep canyons that had to be bridged. To explain how unruly the river is: even great engineer Apollodorus of Damascus, who built the bridge across the Danube and raised Trajan's Column, did not correctly gauge the force of the Tagus River. The ruins of his bridge lie at Alconétar. All that remains of it are six arches. Once it was composed of eighteen arches and was eighteen hundred feet in length.

The bridge of Alcántara was designed with only six gigantic arches. It is six hundred feet long and its greatest height is a hundred fifty feet above the churning waters of the river bed. On the center arch is the date: "Erected in 105 A.D." It was built by Gaius Julius Lacer. On the arch he had engraved the words:

Pontem Perfeci Mansurum in Saecula

which may be read:

I have created a bridge that shall last for ages.

And it has. It has had need of very few repairs through the centuries; its huge granite blocks have never been replaced. Near the head of the bridge on the western side is a temple. Some believe it to have been the mausoleum of Lacer, the builder of the bridge, so that his shade could look over the bridge that he so proudly built. On the bridge is a long list, the names of Romans and Celts who subscribed the funds to the building of the bridge in honor of their emperor, Trajan.

In time, the Romans had their roads bridged so well that a traveler could go all the way from Hadrian's Wall to Brindisi (with the exception of crossing the English channel by ferry-boat), a distance of eighteen hundred miles.

Bridges had to be maintained. They had to withstand flood, frost, sun, and, what is even worse, vibration. The Roman bridges were built for wagons that carried twelve hundred pounds. And yet the Bridge of Augustus, built in

The bridge of Augustus, also attributed to Tiberius, spans the Marecchia River at Rimini. It was built by Augustus in A.D. 9 to move his troops from Rome over the Via Flaminia to Pannonia and Dalmatia.

The aqueduct of Segovia in Spain, constructed of huge blocks of granite without cement, was built in the time of Augustus.

A.D. 9 on the Adriatic coast, across the Marecchia River in Italy, carries today thirty thousand tons of modern traffic. And it is two thousand years old. In America, when iron bridges were being built in 1880 to withstand the traffic of steam engines, bridges collapsed at the rate of twenty a year.

The Romans built for eternity. They had a certain grave solid virtue—a proud, arrogant dignity. To do something was to do it well. When the engineer Frontinus looked over the fourteen aqueducts that brought 2,500,000 gallons of fresh water daily to Rome, he wrote:

". . . you are welcome to compare, if you will, the idle pyramids with them, as well as the useless although famous works of the Greeks."

Some complain that the Roman roads and the Roman bridges were of an unnecessary solidity. But what is wrong with solidity? For a very long time it was felt that the Romans were merely copying the Greeks. That the Greeks were the thinkers, the Romans only the appliers. Nothing could be further from reality. For one thing, the Romans took the road and the bridge out of the mud and gave it life, utility, and beauty. The people built bridges, as shown in the bridge of Alcántara, people built roads; one man on record left his entire fortune for the building of roads in his province. A Roman was proud to have been a builder of a road or a bridge. Listen to what a Greek said about Greece:

"Among the Greeks, members of their government, if they are entrusted with no more than a talent of silver . . . cannot keep their faith . . . whereas among Romans those who are officials and are dealing with large sums of money maintain correct conduct. Whereas it is a rare thing to find a Greek who keeps his hands off public money . . . among the Romans one rarely comes across a man who has been detected in misconduct of this kind . . ."

This is the type of Roman virtue that built the roads and the bridges that have served men for two thousand years.

IX

IMP CAESAR
DIVI NERVAE F
NERVA TRAIANVS
AVG GERM DACIC
PONT MAX TR POT
XIII IMP VI COS V
P P

VIAM A BENEVENTO
BRVNDISIVM PECVN
SVA FECIT

Milestone V on the Benevento-Brindisi road, built by the Emperor Trajan to extend the Via Appia to the southeast coast of Italy

Milestones and Way Stops

A road becomes a road not because someone has trampled down the wayward earth. It becomes a road when it is built and when it is maintained. "If you cannot go back over it," said a Roman, "it is not a road."

The idea of maintenance was quickly grasped by the Romans. As roads grew, so did their use, and traffic on them was ruinous. The Senate created a board of traffic control, whose members were called *curatores viarum*, which superintended the building of the roads as well as their repair.

As the city of Rome grew and trade grew, the traffic brought on bedlam. "Where is sleep possible in Rome?" asked a poet. "The crossing of wagons in the narrow winding streets, the swearing of drivers, brought to a standstill in the traffic, would snatch sleep from a sea-calf or the Emperor himself." And there were hawkers passing along, loudly bartering their packets of sulphur matches or glass trinkets.

Julius Caesar wrote a decree ordering that the stream of people, wagons, beasts of burden, carts, and all else cease using the streets of Rome from sunrise until dusk. But then all that noise at night, it almost makes one shudder to think of it. Finally, the Senate took pause to regulate the traffic.

In 123 B.C. a young nobleman, then tribune of Rome, ordered that all the roads be marked by milestones. Plutarch says that it ". . . was Gaius Gracchus who caused all the roads to be divided into miles." The Roman mile measured a little less than our modern mile. They paced a Roman mile as about 4800 feet and then marked it. The milestone was usually seven feet high, weighed one thousand pounds, and was set into a stone base. It generally was carefully carved to give the name of the emperor under whose reign the road was built or repaired. This one on the Via Traiana is typical:

V

IMP. CAESAR.
DIVI. NERVAE. F.
NERVA. *TRAIANUS.*
AUG. GERM. DACIC.
PONT. MAX. TR. POT.
XIII. IMP. VI. COS. V.
P.
VIAM. A. BENEVENTO.
BRUNDISIUM. PECUN.
SUA. FECIT.

Translated, it is Milestone V, five Roman miles out of Benevento to Brindisi, erected by the Emperor Trajan. Also inscribed are some of his other titles, such as conqueror of Dacia. But mainly it gives the mileage, the name of the road, and the emperor under whose auspices it was built.

The erection of milestones probably came out of the social program undertaken by Gaius Gracchus. He was born in 153 B.C. His mother was Cornelia, the daughter of the great Scipio Africanus, who had defeated Hannibal in Africa. Rome in the time of this young nobleman had suddenly grown fatly rich. There were so many slaves that the Roman peasant could not work on the public lands acquired by the rich. Many people in the lower classes became landless. They drifted into the city. Poverty was extreme.

When night fell over Rome, it was like the shadow of a great danger. Everyone who had a home fled to it, shut himself in, pulled down the shutters, put chains across the door. Shops fell silent. It was at this time that the young Gracchus was elected tribune of the people, an ancient office that had been created to protect the lower classes. Gracchus proposed agricultural and land reforms. He suggested that free Romans be allowed free land in the newly conquered lands of Africa. He even challenged the Senate. So in 121 B.C. he found himself without office, and in the riots that followed he and three thousand others lost their lives.

But before his defeat Gracchus had ordered that all roads be marked with milestones. Perhaps the idea came to him as a means of giving work to the unemployed, for each milestone had to be quarried and transported in a cart. Its place exactly marked one thousand Roman paces from the other. It had to be set in a stone base that was cut to receive the stone. Once set up, it had to be carved and the correct distance marked on it. All this required a tremendous amount of labor.

The Via Domitia, which went into Gaul, was the first road outside Italy to be marked with milestones. One carries a date which would be equivalent to 120 B.C. Distances were recorded from the road to the nearest city, or where the road had its origin.

In Rome, in the Forum, they placed the *Miliarium Aureum* —the Golden Milestone. From this stone, a fragment of which still exists, but not in gold, all roads were measured — so many Roman miles from the Golden Milestone. Still, as roads grew long, hundreds of miles in length, such a system became impractical. By the time of the third century, Rome had 372 roads under its care. These went to the ends of the then known world.

Even the Emperor Augustus, whose mind was a storehouse of information, could not remember all the roads he had seen or built. So he had, as has been related, a map etched in gold which he kept in his bedchamber. Cities were inlaid in precious stones. At any moment he had a dispatch from Pannonia, or Britannia, or Antioch, he could look at his map and find the place mentioned in the letter.

Vespasian, who had commanded a legion in Britain, placed a gigantic road map in the Forum. It was carved in marble with roads and place names. Vespasian, whose origins were humble, never claimed himself to be more than he was: a "frugal, earthy, facetious Italian." After Nero's death there was the "year of the four Emperors." Three had come and gone; Vespasian was the fourth. In the ten years that he was ruler, between A.D. 69 and 79, he undertook many practical works. He reformed the army. Roman coinage after Nero was in a terrible state; Vespasian reorganized it. In Hither Asia he united all the areas by a new road system. In Spain, between A.D. 77 and 79, he began the Via Nova, the "New Road," which ran from Astorga (Asturica Augusta) to Braga (Bracara Augusta) in Portugal.

Then, as he wanted to know what roads went where and to let the people know the same thing, he ordered that the overseer of the Roman roads make the huge map in the Forum. From this large mural map copyists made roll maps for travelers.

By this time there were twenty to thirty public libraries in Rome. The first library was set up by a book lover named Asinius Pollio. At first Romans wrote only for their friends or patrons and their writings were read aloud. But as the public interest grew, so did the new profession of publishing. These book merchants brought together trained teams of expert slaves. Many of them were intelligent men, so they became copyists, or *librarii*. They copied books on papyrus, which was made by laminating strips of the papyrus plant, or on the more expensive parchment from the skin of young goats, treated until it became almost transparent. Books were expensive, since they were all hand-lettered. The art of reading was widespread and the publishers grew rich. Poems written in Rome were carried by ship or by wagon train into the farthest corners of the empire where: ". . . the verses could be recited by some legionnaire in his distant garrison." "But," said a Roman poet, "this did not help my money bag and I knew nothing of it."

The publishers also made copies of the maps of Roman roads for travelers. They were called *itinerarii*. If you wished to journey from Rome to Florence by way of the Via Cassia, the shortest route, you could go down to any of the book-sellers in Rome and find such an *itinerarium*.

The brothers Sosii had a bookshop at the exit of Vicus Tuscus on the Forum behind the Temple of Castor. Horace used to go there to thumb the newly made books. He bought at the Sosiis' an itinerary for his trip when he, in company of others, took the long journey from Rome to Brindisi in 38 B.C., about which he later wrote a satire: *Rome to Brindisi with Stops*. There were others: Dorus, who had copies of Cicero and traveling maps to sell, and Secundus, whose bookstall was not far from the Forum of Peace.

The *itinerarium* that was sold then showed the distances between cities or way stops. It displayed the rivers to be crossed and marked the bridges. Mountains were marked on the maps, and even short cuts. A traveler could calculate with this map the time needed to arrive at his journey's end. Per-

A portion of the Peutinger Table, also known as the world map of Castorius, showing the four roads that led to the city of Capua.

haps there were indications where a good wine or a dish of truffles might be had at some tavern along the way.

All of these road maps have perished. The only surviving *itinerarium* is a famous one in Vienna, the Peutinger Table. It is thought to be an eleventh-century copy of an original made sometime in the third century. It is a map of all of the known Roman military roads from Britain to the Euphrates, from the Rhine to Africa; India and all three Arabias are included. Rivers, mountains, lakes, and seas are put down in six colors. There are many different symbols for buildings, such as a storehouse, called a *horreum*, and a *taberna*, or tavern, where travelers could rest, eat, and drink. Cisterns, where water was held, were always indicated by the word *aquae* (waters), and,

This portion of the map shows a pretorium, *barracks of the Pretorian Guard. Smaller houses are* mansiones *and numerals give distances between cities.*

to be doubly sure that you knew water was there, the artist drew a large building in which there was a reservoir of water, colored blue. Towering lighthouses were so obviously marked that no one could mistake the tall tower with flames and smoke pouring out of it.

A barrack-fortress where the imperial guard lived, the *pretorium*, is clearly differentiated from other buildings, and the word *pretorium* is written above it. Temples, such as the Templum Augusti, were clearly marked so that the traveler would know where he might worship. Harbors are well drawn. One need not be a soothsayer to make out the port of Ostia lying at the mouth of the Tiber. The harbor, the lighthouse, and the storage rooms for cargo, as well as the commercial city of Ostia and the Via Ostiensis that led to it, are easily recognized.

All these and countless other details are contained in this map. It is twenty-one feet long and twelve inches high. It is one of the treasures in the Nationalbibliothek in Vienna.

The Greek poet Aristophanes said that "roads without inns are no better than life without holidays." All Roman roads of any length had halting stations for travelers to rest, for horses to be changed, and for goods to be exchanged. The first organized way stations seem to have been built by the Assyrians as early as 680 B.C. On the road between Susa and Babylon, in Persia, there were official post stations every fifteen miles. Herodotus, the Greek historian who saw these stations, was astonished. The inscription over the main New York Post Office, which begins: *Neither snow nor rain nor heat nor gloom of night stays these couriers . . .* , meaning, of course, to inspire the modern postman, was taken from the history of Herodotus. He was referring to the Persians.

Cyrus the Persian set up the halting stations. Every fifteen miles, more or less, there was a way stop, complete with stables, grooms, horses, and food. But this was only for those who could use the royal road. It was not for the common traveler.

The Greeks got their ideas of road building from the Persians. The Greeks had way stations, yet they were not organized. Their roads were poorly made. "Greek roads," wrote a Greek about his own land, "were easier for me than for mules. They were impassable for carriages."

The Romans were different. They liked things well done. Having ruled the straight line into world thought, they also brought organization into disorganized nature.

There were in general three types of halting stations. The post stations were six to sixteen miles apart, depending on the terrain. These were called the *cursus publici* and were used only by officials. The Emperor Augustus created the office of "overseer of the official post":

"In passports, dispatches, and private letters, the Emperor Augustus used as his seal first a sphinx, then later an image of Alexander the Great. Finally his own, carved on his signet ring by Disocurides. He always attached to his letters not only the day but even the night to say when it was written."

Mail was given to the official postman in a valise. He rode from station to station, changing horses when needed. He was called a *tabellarius* because the letters he carried were often written on wax tablets with a stylus.

The postman wore pants. This was unusual because pants were believed to be worn only by barbarians. He had a warm woolen cloak and a flat headgear called a *petasus*. It is the same that Mercury wore, except that wings were attached to his.

Where the swift-riding postmen changed horses, at the *mutatio*, there were usually twenty or more horses and mules in the stables. There were hostlers, who took care of the forage for the animals, and grooms and postilions who traveled with the larger wagons. Care for the animals was handled by a staff of horse doctors.

How fast could they travel? One hundred miles a day was not unusual. "One was sent," wrote a Roman historian of a postman, "from Aquileia to Rome, changing horses he traveled so swiftly that he reached Rome on the fourth day." And the distance is five hundred miles. When the brother of Tiberius was ill in Germany, Tiberius "traveled 200 Roman miles in 24 hours." Pliny said, "this was a wonderful thing and an instance of incredible celerity."

That was the official post. Private post or that used by merchants, who were denied all of the luxuries given to the royal mail, had a harder time. Cicero, who was a great letter writer, complained that "in the forests of Spain our messengers have always been captured. It has become more dangerous on account of robberies . . . they search our messengers . . . so that unless letters had come by sea I would know nothing of what happens there." Letters were often lost or destroyed, and always delayed. Seneca, who was the tutor of Nero (a thankless task, since he was forced to kill himself at Nero's orders), once wrote: "I received your letter many months after it was sent off . . ."

How one traveled on the Roman roads, then as now, depended on the amount of money in one's purse, or whom one knew. Most Romans who were well connected had friends everywhere, and they would stay at their villas when traveling from place to place.

For the less favored there were the *mansiones* at intervals of twenty miles or so. These seem to have been built by the local community and kept up by local taxes. By law the keeper of the resthouse had to arrange rooms for the traveler and have food on hand. These were state-controlled.

Near the *mansiones* were the inns called *tabernae*. They were, one gathers from the things people said of them, not always the nicest places to roost. They were put up and run by people of the lower classes, sometimes a soldier who had served out his years in the army. Here beds were provided, mules and horses stabled, and food, wine, or mead offered. All sorts of people mingled here: local farmers, old soldiers, postmen, drovers who came in with their big, creaking wagons, muleteers, and travelers. One can imagine what such a place was like. At one end of the room an open fireplace, where a pot of soup or stew might be cooking or bread baking, and servant girls bringing in wine. All the while men filling the place with their coarse talk.

Yet not all the *tabernae* were like this. Some were famous, like the Three Taverns, on the Via Appia. It was famous for its bread and cheese. Paul of Tarsus stayed there on his way to Rome. And farther along the Via Appia was an even more famous one called the Tabernae Caediciae. It was named after its owner. Horace stayed there. There were many others.

The importance of these way stops was that they enabled people to travel long distances. It gave them a place to stay. It made travel possible. More important still, around the taverns grew settlements known as *canabae*. Innkeepers brought in wine sellers. Then a wheelwright appeared to repair wagons, then a blacksmith, a horse doctor. Then a mill to grind flour for bread, and dealers in the spoils of war. Soon the *canabae* grew into villages, then the villages into towns. This is the origin of a number of now famous cities. Many of the cities that stand along the Rhine and the Danube, such as Cologne, Mainz, Strasbourg, Vienna, and Budapest, began as *tabernae*.

The army walked, the knights rode, the emperor traveled in a splendid four-wheeled wagon called a *raeda*.

The *raeda* was pulled by two or four horses and it had two postilions to operate it. It was splendidly ornamented inside and out. It had space enough for a whole family. There was even a larger carriage, called the *carruca*. It was a sleeping carriage. Inside was a splendid bed with pillows and coverings. Blinds closed off the light. The historian Pliny traveled in such a conveyance. He traveled widely. He served as a cavalry officer in Germany, then he practiced law in Rome; he made innumerable trips to most of Rome's overseas colonies, during which time he wrote over fifty books. He ended up as an admiral of the fleet. Pliny liked to read, and to dictate to his secretary as he traveled. So for Pliny, the booksellers made special pocket editions or, better, rolls, for the Roman books were rolled rather than bound in pages. A *carruca* such as the one in which Pliny traveled could cover fifteen to twenty Roman miles a day.

The Romans also employed the *cisium*. This was an elegant two-wheeled cab. Very light and swift, it held two people and was capable of covering more than twenty-five miles a day. The last in the line of travel vehicles was the solid-wheeled cart. It had four wheels and was pulled by two or four oxen. These were the moving vans of the empire. These were the wagons, capable of transporting fifteen hundred pounds, that left deep ruts in the flagstones of the Roman roads. Roman roads everywhere show the grooves these solid wheels wore in the hard pavement of the road.

Of all these types of conveyances we have a full record. There are countless illustrations of them left to us on tombs, sarcophagi, mosaics, and wall paintings.

Roads and communications, travel and accommodations made Roman civilization possible. These in turn made possible what Pliny called "the boundless majesty of the Pax Romana."

X

The Golden Milestone in the Forum in Rome

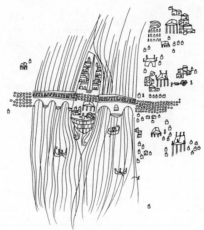

Terminus—

"You are on your own."

Anno Domini 410.
"From the Senate of Rome to all consuls, tribunes, and praetors. The devastations of Alaric the Barbarian have destroyed imperial Rome, burnt its records, and ransacked its treasuries. You can no longer rely on Rome for finance or direction. *You are on your own.*"

The end had been long in coming.

The dying Emperor Hadrian seemed to have a vision of it. "Catastrophe and ruin will fall one day on Rome . . ." But the final "catastrophe and ruin" took a long time in coming. Precisely 272 years after Hadrian's death the curtain came down on one of the greatest empires the world has ever known.

Rome had had a long line of dedicated rulers from the time of Nerva in A.D. 96 to the end of the rule of Marcus Aurelius. When Marcus Aurelius died on the banks of the

167

Roman ruins in Tunisia

Danube River, at the Roman outpost of Vindobona, now called Vienna, on May 17, A.D. 180, it marked the end of a long century of progress.

"All of the world's people," said a poet, "are entwined under a single name—Romans. They are world citizens who share a common law. All are Roman citizens, peers in their world. They are Roman citizens whether they live in Africa or in Hither Asia or if they live on the banks of the Rhine River. All look to Rome. There is a single coinage. There is a single law. There are no frontiers. No major customs barriers. Travel is open and free. On the Roman roads, police guard against highwaymen; inns, taverns, and halting stations are open to all."

Travel, while slow and ofttimes uncomfortable by our present standards, was faster by land than anything that latter-day men invented, that is until the advent of railroads.

"In every deed," said a Greek poet, "Rome has made *real* Homer's dictum—that the earth is the property of all.

"You, Rome, have measured the whole world. You have spanned the rivers with bridges . . . tunneled through mountains to make level roads. You have filled desolate places with farms and made life easier by seeing that two things are supplied: law and order.

"Everywhere, O Rome, you have erected temples, gateways, schools, factories, aqueducts, fountains, and gymnasiums. It could be said in truth that the world which from the beginning has been working under an illness has now been put in the way of health . . . Cities are radiant in their splendor and their grace, and the whole world is as trim as a garden . . ."

The Roman world, to be sure, was not all that good. Yet much of what the poet sang was in essence true. The Roman world, "as trim as a garden," however, did have a few strangling weeds; the worst was Commodus, son of Marcus Aurelius. With him began Rome's decline and fall.

According to the Roman historian Dio Cassius, "Commodus was a greater plague to the Romans than any pestilence or crime. He wanted to change the name of Rome and call it 'Commodiana' after himself. He wanted to have the title of Hercules. A statue of gold weighing a thousand pounds representing himself in combat with a bull was cast. He entered the arena to fight gladiators: he was armed with a sword and they only with a women's wooden weaving batten. He surpassed all others in lust, greed, and cruelty; he kept faith with no one." If a time can be fixed for the decline of the Roman Empire, it was the rule of Commodus. A wrestler whom he had wounded throttled him in his bath; the date was A.D. 192.

Severus the African, who became emperor in A.D. 193, tried to stop Rome's decline. He was not of royal blood. He had no claims to be emperor except that he was a good military commander. He was born in the year 146 at Leptis Magna. He had studied rhetoric in Carthage, law in Greece, and had served long and well in the army. He had African blood, and while he spoke Latin perfectly himself, he was always embarrassed by his sister, who spoke Latin with a Libyan accent. He married a Syrian lady called Julia Domna.

Remains of a Roman bridge at Foz de Lumbier in Spain

The triumphal arch of Sbeitla, built in the third century
after Septimius Severus was proclaimed emperor

First Severus looked to his native land. On the occasion of his return there, people in all of the splendid cities in Algeria, Tunisia, and Libya erected monuments to him. He lavished money on their cities, he repaired the roads, he built a defense line of forts, called the Limes Severiana, to keep out the desert people. Finally, on the coins bearing his portrait he had struck on the obverse side a date palm, a symbol of Libya, and on top of it the word "Africa."

Then he led his troops to fight in Hither Asia, on the Rhine, and against the tribes on the Danube. Meanwhile he reorganized the Roman post office. He saw that laws were passed to protect the poor. He erected, in the Forum of Rome, the last triumphal arch to be erected there; he repaired and built roads.

One road bears his name. It will be recalled that the old

Via Appia, when it reached the sea at Terracina, turned southward. The seacoast between Terracina and Ostia had no road. Severus ordered that a road be built, and he paid for it out of his own funds. It was a difficult road to build. The area was full of swamps, since the water of the Pontine Marshes seeped into it. In fact, there was so much water there that Nero, when he was kept from song and declaiming, had a plan to dig a canal from Ostia to Terracina. The road is a marvel of engineering. Parts of the Via Severiana, as it was and still is called, can be seen marching under the umbrella pines on the coast. It can be seen entering the ruins of Ostia at the south gate and can be clearly seen running between buildings that were once a Jewish synagogue.

The Via Severiana was the last road of any size to be built in the Roman Empire. It was dedicated in the year 208, but Septimius Severus never saw it. He was then in England, repairing Hadrian's Wall, fighting the Picts and the climate. He died at York, England, in the year 211.

As he was dying he called to him his two grown sons. He asked that they share the burdens of the empire together and admonished the two, Caracalla and Geta, to ". . . live in peace with each other." Saying, "I have been everything: orator, lawyer, consul, tribune, general, emperor; I have been everything, and everything in vain," he died.

"Live in peace with each other . . ." Even on the London-Rome road "there was," said a historian, "friction between them . . . they did not even use the same inns together." Caracalla did not let much time go by, for once in Rome he sought out his brother, killed him, and became sole emperor in the year 212.

Caracalla built the immense baths in Rome that bear his name. He repaired the roads in Spain, he repaved a road 110 miles in length that led to what is now Augsburg in Germany, he built another road to a place called Villa Magna, at his own cost. Before he was murdered at the road junction of Carrhae, in what is now Turkey, he had ruled for six years.

Decline continued.

There was the period of the "Thirty Tyrants." In fifty years there were no less than twenty-six recognized emperors. One ruled for five years. That was an exception. Others lasted for weeks, some for days; one was emperor for a mere two hours. Many were murdered.

One can picture what this misrule did to roads and communications. As the people depended on wheat brought from Africa and Egypt, the broken roads had their effect on transport and hunger.

Diocletian came to power in the year 284. He was a soldier, born in Dalmatia, in present-day Yugoslavia. When he was elected emperor by the Roman legions, he divided the administration of the empire and made Maximian, who also came from Dalmatia, Caesar, then Augustus, and put him in charge of the west. His headquarters were at Milan. Maximian made an inspection trip into Gaul. This splendid Roman province had been overrun and made desolate by repeated invasions.

It was true, the Caesar reported: "After the fork of the road that led to Augustodunum [Autun] everything was desolate, uncared for; all was rank, mute, and dismal. Even the military roads . . . they were so much in disrepair that only half-loaded or empty carts could go over it . . ."

During the time that Diocletian was emperor, between the years 284 and 305, he did all he could to stop the dry rot in the empire. He repaired roads in Spain and France. He tried to curb the cost of living. He made a list and fixed the prices for all goods and services. "Is anyone so dull and unfeeling as not to know, not to have seen . . . the high prices in our markets . . . I will decree capital punishment, that is death, to anyone who charges more than these prices . . ."

Then when Diocletian found that he could do no more, he abdicated as emperor. On May 1, 305, he retired to his palace at Split (Spalatum), in Yugoslavia (it still stands mostly intact). Diocletian was the only emperor in one hundred years to leave the principate alive. After a period of civil war, Constantine became emperor in 306.

Constantine, surnamed the Great, apart from his services to Christianity, did well for the empire. He prevented the barbarians from coming into Italy, and Rome knew the first prolonged peace in a century. So as to organize the state better he created the Eastern Empire and built his capital at Constantinople. To keep communications open with Rome and the Western Empire, he made extensive repairs on the Via Egnatia. This road, which began at Aquileia at the end of the Adriatic Sea, close to modern Venice, went down the rugged coast of Yugoslavia, cut inland through the mountainous terrain, passed Hadrianopolis, and so on to Constantinople. Constantine raised his own monument, the Arch of Constantine, close to the Colosseum in Rome. In the year 337 he died. In doing so he dedicated Rome to chaos.

One wonders how Rome kept itself together in the next century. War was constant. Emperors came and went as fast as the returning four seasons.

The death throes of Rome began in 406. Hordes of barbarians—Franks, Suevi, Vandals, Alans, Burgundians, Visigoths, Ostrogoths—fell upon Gaul, Spain, North Africa, and Italy. The Romanized towns were destroyed. In Britain, Roman troops had been withdrawn and Roman rule came to an end there almost 450 years after the landing of Julius Caesar.

Alaric, the Goth, appeared in 408. His armies devastated

Constantine the Great,
Roman emperor A.D. *306-337*

Northern Italy and what was left of Gaul. Then he moved on
Rome, spreading terror all the way. At that moment a young
pagan poet, Rutilius, was on his way home to Gaul. He had
been in Rome, now he dared not even return by land. On the
ship he wrote his bitter poem *On My Journey Home*:

> O Rome!
>> Listen, fairest queen in all the world.
> You are welcomed among the stars of heaven, mother of
>> men
>> And mother of the gods.
> To you we sing praise
>> And ever shall.
> So long as the fates allow,
>> None can be wholly forgetful of you. Your works

leading to one's city; the better the roads the more easily the cities could be attacked and sacked.

In time the roads of what was once the Roman Empire were all but gone. A traveler who went along the remains of the great Via Argenta in Spain said that to travel over the road, one had to have "a falcon's eyes, an ass's ears, a monkey's face, a merchant's words, a camel's back, a hog's mouth, a deer's feet . . ." to get to the journey's end.

In these lands roads were once so extensive that they could have girthed the earth twice—now they were gone. Soon destroyed, for lack of care, were more than half of the two thousand bridges that once spanned all the rivers, culverts, and canyons within the Roman Empire. Gone was the time when a man coming out from London could cross the Channel and make his way to Rome without once wetting his feet. Gone were the inns and halting stations that appeared at stated intervals along the roads. Missing now were the guidebooks, the maps, the itineraries that told the traveler the distances of travel. The wonderful road system was gone. There was to be nothing like it again for fifteen hundred years.

XI

CHRONOLOGICAL TABLE OF ROMAN ROAD BUILDING

A SELECTED BIBLIOGRAPHY

INDEX

DATE	POLITICAL EVENT	ROAD BUILDING
B.C.		
753	Legendary founding of Rome	
ca. 450		Roads existing (possibly only as tracks): Via Latina, Via Salaria, Via Appia, Via Flaminia, Via Cassia, and Via Clodia
390	Gauls sack Rome	
ca. 350		Via Latina goes to Mt. Algidus and to Liri Valley as a *via vicina*
350	Campania becomes part of Rome	
327	Second Samnite War	Lime mortar, cement, introduced to Magna Graecia
312		Censor Appius Claudius builds the Via Appia
ca. 300	Etruria absorbed by Rome	
267	Brindisi captured by Rome	
241	Sicily ceded to Rome at end of First Punic War	Via Aurelia built from Rome to Pisa
220	Gaius Flaminius censor	Via Flaminia begun to Fano and Rimini
218	Hannibal crosses the Alps; victor over the Romans at the River Trebbia	
210		Via Valeria begun in Sicily
187		M. Aemilius Lepidus builds the Via Aemilia from Rimini to Piacenza through Bologna
177		Old track from Rome to Arezzo rebuilt, became Via Cassia
149–146	Third Punic War; Carthage destroyed	Via Postumia built to serve Genoa, Piacenza, Cremona, and Aquileia; Via Aemilia extended to Piacenza and Tortona (Dertona)
148–132		Via Flaminia extended along the Adriatic to Aquileia and Brindisi
ca. 145		Via Egnatia built from Yugoslavia to Greece; first stone bridge built across the Tiber
ca. 140–125		Via Cassia reaches Florence and Pisa
132		Old gravel track rebuilt and named Via Popillia, goes from Capua to Reggio (Rhegium)
123	Gaius Gracchus tribune	Erects milestones on all roads
109		Via Aemilia Scauri built to continue Via Aurelia; Genoa-Tortona road improved
77		Pompey builds road over Cottian Alps (Alpes Cottiae) from Turin to Vienne in France
60	First Triumvirate: Caesar, Pompey, Crassus	
58	Caesar begins conquest of Gaul	
57		Caesar improves road over Great St. Bernard Pass

ROMAN ROAD BUILDING

DATE	POLITICAL EVENT	ROAD BUILDING
49	Caesar crosses the Rubicon	
44	Caesar murdered; Octavian consul	New law forbidding wheeled traffic in Rome
27	Octavian emperor	Repairs whole of Via Flaminia
20		Little St. Bernard Pass repaired
15	Campaign of Tiberius and Drusus in the Alps	Drusus builds new road over Reschen Scheideck Pass between Adige and Inn valleys
1		Via Augusta rebuilt between Narbonne (Narbo Martius) and Cadiz
A.D.		
3		Via Sebaste built in Turkey
11–16	Germanicus' campaign against Germans	Road built in Africa Proconsularis between Gabès and Tebessa (Theveste)
24–25		Via Argenta built from Mérida to Salamanca
41–54	Claudius emperor	Repairs Via Augusta
43	Britain conquered by Claudius	Work begun on port at Ostia; Via Ostiensis rebuilt
44		First part of Watling Street in Britain paved and extended to St. Albans
47		Claudius builds road through Brenner Pass
54	Claudius murdered; Nero emperor	
54–59		Nero repairs the Via Augusta and the Via Argenta in Spain
64	Great fire in Rome; first persecutions of Christians	
75		Road built in Africa from Bône (Hippo) to Tebessa
77–79		Vespasian builds the Via Nova from Astorga to Braga
79	Eruption of Vesuvius; Pompeii and Herculaneum buried	
ca. 80		Via Domitiana built from Sinuessa to Naples
81	Colosseum completed in Rome	
98	Nerva dies; Trajan emperor	Via Nerva begun in North Africa
98–117		New road built by Trajan in Egypt from Qift (Coptos) to Berenice
ca. 100	Greatest extent of Roman Empire	Building of amphitheaters in Nîmes and Arles; Maison Carrée built in Nîmes; triumphal arches in Carpentras and Orange
104		Bridge over Danube built by Apollodorus
104–106	Conquest of Dacia; becomes Roman province	
114		Via Traiana, from Benevento to Brindisi, begun

DATE	POLITICAL EVENT	ROAD BUILDING
121		Hadrian reinforces the *limes* along the Rhine
122–127		Hadrian's Wall built in Britain
123		New road built in Africa Proconsularis from Tebessa to Carthage
125		Hadrian overhauls the Via Cassia
138	Hadrian dies; Antoninus Pius emperor	
180	Marcus Aurelius dies; Commodus emperor	
193	Septimius Severus emperor	
197		Via Severiana built to connect Terracina with Ostia
211	Death of Septimius Severus; Caracalla emperor	
214		Caracalla rebuilds roads in Spain
271	Aurelian emperor; begins wall around Rome	
284–305	Diocletian emperor	
306–337	Constantine emperor	
317–323		Constantine rebuilds Via Nova in Spain
330	Constantinople established as second Roman capital	
337	Constantine dies	
364		Valentinian I rebuilds the Via Augusta in Spain
410	Central government advises all governors in all provinces that help from Rome has ended	

A Selected Bibliography

There is no problem about the selection of literature that deals specifically with the Roman roads, since there is no single book about the Roman road system available. The first attempt to write such a book was made in 1626 by Nicolas Bergier. A French lawyer, he wrote *Histoire des grands chemins de l'Empire Romain*. His book was based on Roman inscriptions and classical history. The next attempt was made by Konrad Miller in 1916. His *Itineraria Romana,* written in German, is based on a copy of the ancient Roman road map and on modern and classical literature. Both books are technical, both are difficult to obtain.

Ashby, T. *The Roman Campagna in Classical Times*. London, 1927. A book by one of the best-known British archaeologists, long resident in Italy, whose work was most thorough and authoritative.

De Camp, L. Sprague. *Ancient Engineers*. New York, 1963. An excellent book on ancient techniques. The Roman section, pp. 164-259, is very detailed.

Forbes, R. J. *Notes on the History of Ancient Roads and Their Construction*. Amsterdam, 1934.

Grant, Michael, and Pottinger, Don. *Romans*. Edinburgh, 1960.

Gregory, J. W. *The Story of the Road*. London, 1938.

Hagen, J. *Die Romerstrassen in der Rheinprovinz*. Bonn, 1932. A very complete book on Roman roads in Germany, mostly on the Rhine, based on physical research and literature. Available in German only.

Harrison, David. *Along Hadrian's Wall*. London, 1962. A detailed study of the Roman wall in northern England and the roads that led to it and about it.

Jenison, Madge. *Roads*. London, 1949. A little-known but stimulating study of roads everywhere. Much on the Romans.

Margary, Ivan. *Roman Roads in Britain*. 2 vols. London, 1955 and 1957. A description of Roman roads throughout Britain and an exhaustive study of their history and technology.

Miller, Konrad. *Die Peutingersche Tafel*. Stuttgart, 1962. A reprint of Konrad Miller's earlier work on the Roman map of the world. Written in German, but valuable as a teaching aid to be read with this book, since it gives a reproduction of the Roman world map in color.

Mooney, W. W. *Travel Among the Ancient Romans*. Boston, 1920.

Rose, A. C. "Via Appia in the Days When All Roads Led to Rome," Smithsonian Institution, *Annual Report of Board of Regents*. Washington, 1935.

Singer, Charles. (ed.). *A History of Technology*, Vol. II, pp. 500-516. London, 1956. A short chapter, but with very accurate description of Roman roads, bridges, and building techniques.

Ward-Perkins, J. B., and Frederiksen, M. W. *The Ancient Road*. London, 1957. Systems of Central and Northern Ager Faliscus. Papers of the British School of Rome, Vol. XXV (n.s. Vol. XXI). A detailed study of the Via Amerina (an offshoot of the Via Cassia): a minute description of every tomb, bridge, milestone, and the Via Amerina itself. For supplementary reading with this book. It explains the great amount of material still to be found and the need for the study of Roman roads and communications.

Wiseman, F. J. *Roman Spain*. London, 1956. A compact, well-written, and generally useful book on the Romans in Spain. Contains many references to Roman roads in Spain.

Index

185

PHOTO ACKNOWLEDGMENTS

Fratelli Alinari   pp. 119, 133

The Bettmann Archive, Inc.   p. 132

George Holton   pp. 77, 82, 91

The Metropolitan Museum of Art   pp. 107, 117, 175

The New York Public Library   pp. 127, 138

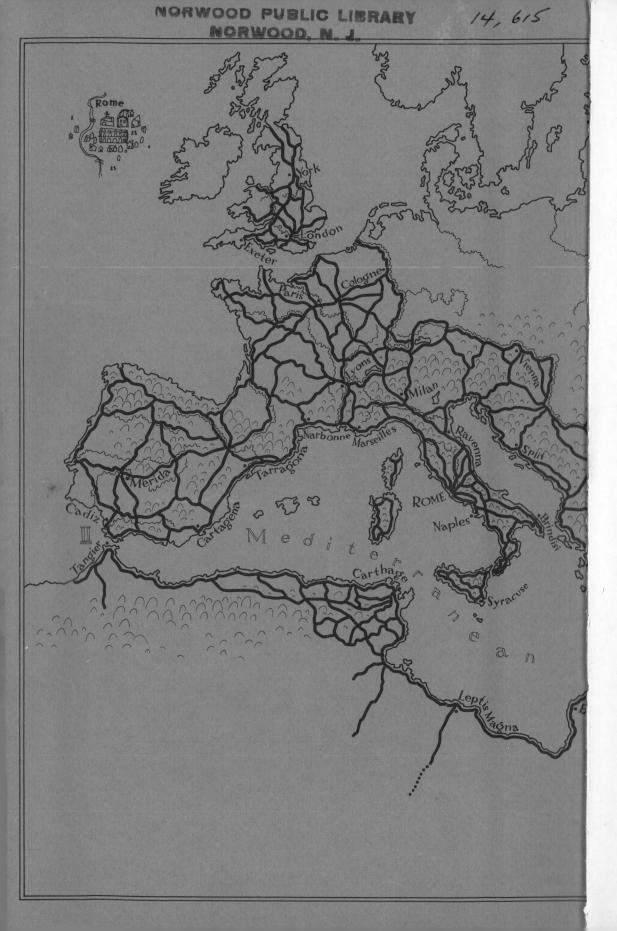

ABOUT THE AUTHOR

VICTOR W. VON HAGEN was born in St. Louis, Missouri. He was twenty-three when he went on his first expedition, to Mexico, and since then he has traveled throughout most of Central and South America. He has become a recognized authority on the great Indian cultures of this hemisphere. After extensively researching the ancient Inca highway system in Peru, Mr. von Hagen turned to Rome and an investigation of the ancient Roman road system. He is director of the Roman Road Expedition and between intervals of exploration lives in Rome with his two young daughters, Adriana and Bettina.

ABOUT THE PHOTOGRAPHER

ADOLFO TOMEUCCI lives in Rome where he was born. A deep interest in ancient Etruscan and Roman history, acquired at the University of Rome, led him to the Roman Road Expedition. He has served the expedition as photographer for the past two years.

ABOUT THE ARTIST

STANISLAO DINO RIGOLO lives with his wife and small son, Marco Antonio, in Tarquinia, Italy, in a medieval house with a 1000-year-old tower. A Canadian citizen, born in Porcia, Italy, Mr. Rigolo has produced animated films for the National Film Board of Canada. At present he is a designer of visual aids for the Food and Agricultural Organization of the United Nations in Rome.

74